Shar-Pei

The Owner's Guide from Puppy to Old Age

Choosing, Caring for, Grooming, Health, Training and Understanding Your Chinese Shar-Pei Dog or Puppy

By Alex Seymour

Copyright and Trademarks

Disclaimer and Legal Notice

views expressed within them. CWP Publishing takes no responsibility for, and will not be liable for, the websites being temporarily unavailable or being removed from the Internet.

The accuracy and completeness of information provided herein and opinions stated herein are not guaranteed or warranted to produce any particular results, and the advice and strategies contained herein may not be suitable for every individual. The author shall not be liable for any loss incurred as a consequence of the use and application, directly or indirectly, of any information presented in this work. This publication is designed to provide information in regard to the subject matter covered.

Neither the author nor the publisher assume any responsibility for any errors or omissions, nor do they represent or warrant that the ideas, information, actions, plans, or suggestions contained in this book are in all cases accurate. It is the reader's responsibility to find advice before putting anything written in this book into practice. The information in this book is not intended to serve as legal advice.

Photo Credit: Joy & Richard Bayliss of Tianshan Shar Pei and owner Russell Sheehan

Foreword

Many of the world's top breeders have been involved in contributing to this book and once you've read this book, you will have all the information you need to make a well-informed decision about whether or not the Shar-Pei is the breed for you.

As an owner, expert trainer and professional dog whisperer, I would like to teach you the human side of the equation, so you can learn how to think more like your dog and eliminate behavioral problems with your pet.

The Chinese Shar-Pei, once a rare dog in the Western world, has gained enormous popularity in recent years. Almost human-like, they are incredibly smart, intuitive and comical at times!

These sturdy, stoic dogs appear calm and confident at first glance. Aloof with strangers, but deeply devoted to their humans, the Shar-Pei garners accolades for being clean, easily housebroken, and quiet.

This is not, however, a breed without drawbacks, and a first-time dog owner needs to be fully aware of all possible health issues. Most Shar-Pei mind their own business unless provoked, but they can be highly territorial with other dogs, and in some cases predatory with cats. In a rural setting, unless properly contained, the breed's ancient hunting instincts may surface.

Perhaps the greatest challenge of the Shar-Pei is his stubborn dominance of the world around him. If you don't have the capacity to be the "alpha" in your household, your Shar-Pei will immediately become the leader of the pack and do as he pleases. To be a successful Shar-Pei owner, you must be able to forge a relationship predicated on mutual respect.

Many enjoy cuddling, but they are too big to be lap dogs. They don't like to be petted on the head by a stranger, because, for the most part, they cannot look up due to the heavily wrinkled eyebrow. Adults or children need to be taught to approach a Shar-Pei by touching them under the chin.

All breeds need crate training, because that helps teach them their boundaries, and the Shar-Pei are certainly no exception. They do not need a great deal of exercise, however, and can live happily in an apartment so long as they get a 20-minute walk per day. When well-trained and well-behaved, the breed is a loyal and highly enjoyable companion.

The information in this book will help you to form a fuller sense of what life with a Shar-Pei would be like, and arm you with the correct questions to ask in your discussions with breeders. No pet purchase should be undertaken without careful consideration. This is particularly true for a breed as special, and at times enigmatic, as the Shar-Pei.

Photo Credit: Lynn and Michael Olds of Lava Kennels Chinese Shar-Pei

Acknowledgments

In writing this book, I also sought tips, advice, photos and opinions from many experts of the Shar-Pei breed.

In particular I wish to thank the following wonderful experts for going out of their way to help and contribute to the book:

USA & CANADA

Cate Stewart of Nordic Star Shar-Pei
nordicstarcsp@yahoo.com

Bobbie Libman of Mikobi Shar-Pei
http://www.sharpeidogs.ca/mikobi

Lauren J Alexander of Lauren's Shar-Pei
http://www.lasharpei.com

Bonnie Stoney of Stoneys Chinese Shar-Pei
bstoney@earthlink.net

Linda J.M. Tintle, D.V.M.
Wurtsboro Veterinary Clinic
163 Sullivan Street, P.O. Box 910
Wurtsboro, New York 12790
845-888-4884
wvc@warwick.net
http://www.wvc.vetsuite.com

Susanna Björnsson of Brekkukots Shar-Pei
http://www.brekkukots.com/

Georgette Schaefer of Yu Kou Shar-Pei
ghschaef@gmail.com

Acknowledgments

Andrea Robins of Gumby's Chinese Shar-Pei Perm Reg'd
http://www.gumbysurprise.com

Barbara & Stephen LaVere of Tzo Wen Shar-Pei
http://www.tzowen.com/

Kathy Probst of Conrad Knoll Shar-Pei
conradknol@aol.com

Lynn and Michael Olds of Lava Kennels Chinese Shar-Pei
http://www.lavakennels.com/

Deena Harvey of Harvs Shar-Pei
http://www.harvssharpei.com/

Kathy Torres & Marie Bradley of Maka Chinese Shar-Pei
http://makacsp.ambercreek.net/

Marilyn Vinson of China Fleet Shar-Pei

Dee Dee Wells of Margem Hills Shar-Pei
http://margemhills.com/

Judy Dorough of Tuj's Chinese Shar-Pei
http://www.tujschineseshar-pei.com

UNITED KINGDOM

Joy & Richard Bayliss of Tianshan Shar-Pei
http://www.tianshansharpei.co.uk/

Claire Davis of Deakie Shar-Pei
http://deakie.com/

Table of Contents

Table of Contents

Table of Contents

Table of Contents

Chapter 1 – Meet the Chinese Shar-Pei

The Chinese Shar-Pei is one of the most distinct and easily recognized of all dog breeds. That very uniqueness explains their growing popularity, but this is not the dog for everyone.

Although they may look like a soft mass of wrinkles, their coat can be harsh and bristly to the point of causing skin irritations in some sensitive individuals. There are three different coat types: horse coats, brush coats and bear coats. Both horse coats and brush coats should have a harsh coat. Bear coats have very fluffy, dense coats similar to Chow Chows.

Horse coats are a little less commonly seen in the show ring; however, they are both judged equally. One is not preferred over the other. Some prefer brush coat, some people prefer horse coat.

The dogs are extremely stubborn and, if not well socialized, can be territorial and aggressive. If a Shar-Pei doesn't want to do something, they won't! At the same time, however, they are incredibly intelligent, and extremely loyal and devoted. If you know what you're getting into, having a Shar-Pei in your life can be a superb experience.

They are one of the easiest dogs to groom, requiring an occasional quick brush and muzzle wipe. As most rarely smell, they need infrequent bathing – you just need to wipe out their ears once every few weeks.

The History of the Shar-Pei

Although an ancient breed, the true origins of the Chinese Shar-Pei are poorly documented, in part because all records regarding the country's canine population were destroyed in 225 BC. The Chinese bred dogs as companions, but also as sources of meat, pelts, and leather.

An interesting fact is there are a few breeds that most closely resemble the wolf genetically. A genetic study has revealed that two branches of the canine family tree were the earliest to diverge from the wolves. One branch includes the oriental breeds Shar-Pei, Shiba Inu, Chow Chow and Akita; the other, the seemingly diverse breeds of African Basenji, Siberian Husky, Alaskan Malamute, Afghan Hound and Saluki. In addition to these ancient dogs, three other groups were developed later, including canines for guarding, herding and hunting.

The Shar-Pei can be traced with some certainty to tomb statues and vases from the Han Dynasty (206 BC – 220 AD). Most experts agree that the Chow Chow figures in the Shar-Pei genetic history, in part because both dogs have a unique bluish black tongue. The Tibetan Mastiff is also a likely ancestor, as is the Great Pyrenees, a breed with double dew claws that sometimes appear in the Shar-Pei as well (although rarely). But the most direct line of descent is believed to be from the Dah Let fighting dog.

The modern Shar-Pei shares many of the same physical characteristics of the Dah Let. Both have powerful jaws and a stiff coat uncomfortable to the mouth of an opponent. Shar-Pei intentionally stiffen their coats as a means of defense. The highly flexible skin in both dogs allows them to maneuver and turn, easily breaking another dog's hold. The skin's spongy, thick texture protects the tissue underneath. If the skin is cut it will excrete mucin, which is the consistency of egg whites; this helps seal and heal the skin. The breed's tiny ears give an attacker little to grab, while still covering the opening.

There are various theories bandied about, one being that the original horse coat Shar-Pei was indigenous to Southern China, where it is warmer, and the brush coat variety comes from Northern China, where it is colder, and that at one time the horse coat Shar-Pei was crossed with a Chow, that is how the coats got longer. The truth is there is currently no hard evidence to prove this speculation.

Dog fighting was one of the only means of entertainment for people living in small, rural villages and on farms. Images of fighting dogs are found throughout Chinese art, but the modern Shar-Pei is not a fighter unless he is seriously provoked.

In China, all dogs that protected property were called "fighting" dogs, but the Shar-Pei was actually more multi-faceted, serving as a home guardian and a hunting animal, but not a retriever. The Shar-Pei instinctively shakes anything it catches, unless the habit is broken through training. Shar-Pei are extremely versatile and have excelled in agility, performance, herding and retrieving.

After 1949, the Communists imposed heavy fines for anyone keeping dogs. The animals were seen as luxury items. Mao Tse-tung ordered mass killings, decimating the canine populations in cities. In the outlying districts, a few Shar-Pei survived and were smuggled out of the country in the 1950s. Concerted efforts to save and promulgate the breed began in the 1970s, principally by C. M. Chung and Matgo Law.

As many existing specimens as possible were relocated to Hong Kong, where a breeding program was established. At this stage of the breed's preservation, all available bloodlines and inbreeding were used to produce consistent dogs from which a breed standard could be developed.

In 1966, a puppy bred by Chung, a male named Lucky, was exported to the United States. A total of five dogs came to America by 1967, but the breed generated little interest.

In 1973, Matgo Law wrote an article for *Dogs* magazine entitled "Chinese Fighting Dogs," in which he expressed concern about the fate of the rare Shar-Pei breed. Imports to the United States increased markedly. In 1974, the Chinese Shar-Pei Club of America (CSPCA) organized to discuss registering the breed with the American Kennel Club.

The first specialty show was held in 1978. By 1982, a new standard was approved that removed any references to the Chow Chow and to fighting dogs. The American Kennel Club accepted the breed in its Miscellaneous Class in 1988. In 1992, the breed entered the Non-Sporting Group and the first Shar-Pei gained a championship title.

In 1981 Heather Ligget imported a fawn male Shar-Pei, Heathstyle Dandelion, from the United States to Great Britain.

Later in the year, Ligget imported a female from Hong Kong, Down-Homes Junoesque.

These dogs produced the first litter of Shar-Pei puppies in the UK. In 1982, fourteen Shar-Pei were registered with The Kennel Club, which recognized the Chinese Shar-Pei Club of Great Britain in 1986.

In 1987 the first Shar-Pei Open Show was held in concert with the Rare Breeds Spectacular. The Crufts Dog Show scheduled Shar-Pei breed classes in 1990, and the Kennel Club allowed the dogs to compete for the title of champion in 1999.

The greatest number of Shar-Pei are found in the United States and Great Britain, but the dogs are slowly gaining in number around the world. The breed is still actively cultivated in Hong Kong, and is now well established in Japan, Germany, Australia, Canada, New Zealand and South America.

Physical Characteristics of the Shar-Pei

The Shar-Pei's unique looks account for much of this breed's popularity, even though the dogs have many endearing characteristics. A Shar-Pei, due to its ease of housebreaking, adaptability and their devotion to the family, can be a good choice for most people; however, it is imperative for any owner, especially a first-time dog owner, to be aware of the potential health problems and how to recognize and treat them. Some of these potential health issues can be very expensive to treat. If a person isn't able to afford proper treatment, this isn't the breed for them. In addition, all owners, and again especially first-time dog owners, must commit to a regular program of socializing their Shar-Pei puppy.

It's hard not to fall instantly in love with a Shar-Pei. The Chinese Shar-Pei Club of Great Britain publishes a magazine called *The Wrinkle*, which aptly describes the dogs themselves. A Shar-Pei looks like one continuous mass of wrinkles with a big head, well-padded muzzle, and lovable frown.

They are not a heavily built breed. They are a moderate breed of moderate bone; they are squarely built, muscular, and strong dogs. Males are larger than females, averaging 55-65 lbs. (25-29 kg) compared to 30-55 lbs. (18-25 kg). The standard in both the United States and the UK calls for the dogs to stand 18-20 inches at the withers. All have the characteristic blue-black tongue, a color that extends to the gums and roof of the mouth – with the exception of dilute colors, which have lavender tongues.

Photo Credit: Cate Stewart of Nordic Star Shar-Pei

The most common color is fawn and red fawn. Below are the colors available to use when registering a Shar-Pei with AKC:

- Apricot dilute
- Black
- Blue dilute
- Lilac dilute
- Cream
- Cream dilute
- Brown
- Chocolate dilute
- Red
- Five-point red dilute
- Isabella dilute (silver shading on a dilute-colored dog)
- Black sable
- Cream sable
- Fawn sable
- Red sable

Alternate colors include:

- White
- Blue sable
- Brown sable

Marking/Patterns (these choices are available; however, brindle, white markings, spotted, patterned or pointed are a disqualification in a show dog):

- Mask Sable
- Brindle White Markings
- Spotted on white Saddle pattern
- Pointed (tan or white; cream points)

The tail and the back of the thighs are often lighter. Patches of white and spotting are not allowed in show dogs, however, and neither is the black and tan color pattern.

Some people like their dogs to stand out due to unusual colors, and certain unscrupulous breeders are catering to this demand by breeding Shar-Pei and claiming they are a rare or a new color and thus demanding more money for them. If you are told this or if the color does not exist in the list of available colors, be very suspicious. Even though spotted, brindle, patterned and pointed dogs exist and can be registered as such, they are not correct and do not conform to the AKC standard.

In texture, the coat is short, harsh, and bristly to the point that it can irritate people with sensitive skin. This is not a hypoallergenic breed, and it's important to be certain you will not have this adverse reaction before adopting a Shar-Pei.

The issue of the Shar-Pei undercoat is somewhat contradictory. Undercoat is not mentioned in the AKC standard; although in the current FCI standard it does state no undercoat, nevertheless the reality is some dogs, usually brush coats, have undercoat. The overall length of the hair should be less than 1 inch / 2.54 cm. There are three coat variations:

- **horse coat** - Especially prickly and rough to the touch, typically softer in one direction and stiffer in the other.

- **brush coat** - Slightly longer coat, with a somewhat smoother feel. Brush coats should feel "stiff" when brushed against the lay (Shar-Pei means "sand skin" which denotes a gritty texture rather than soft); otherwise, their coats are lovely and non-irritating. The brush coat should not exceed 1" in length at the withers.

- **bear coat** - Very fluffy, dense coats similar to Chow Chows. The coat is straight and off-standing on the main trunk of the body but generally lies somewhat flatter on the limbs. The length of coat is considered a "Major Fault" in AKC but not a disqualification. For that reason, you don't see them in the conformation ring but you do see them in performance classes.

Bonnie Stoney of Stoneys Chinese Shar-Pei says: "I actually have people who will only buy bear coats, because the bear coat has a 'teddy bear' personality. The three coat lengths in the breed have three distinct personalities as an average. Horse coats tend to be snobs/divas, brush coats are easy going, bear coats are the lovers."

Photo Credit: Lauren J Alexander of Lauren's Shar-Pei

The Shar-Pei tail is never docked and is set very high – a characteristic feature of the Shar-Pei. The lack of a complete tail is sufficient to disqualify a show dog; a low-set tail, while not desirable, doesn't result in disqualification. The tail is rounded, narrows to a fine point, and can curl over the back or to either side. The tail can be straight up in the air as long as the tip points towards the head.

Breeders may or may not remove the dew claws on the dogs' front feet, but removal of the hind dew claws is required. The surgery is typically performed when the puppies are three days old.

Health and Lifespan

The age of this breed varies greatly. In a healthy dog (not stricken by renal failure, cancer or other serious disease) one can expect a range of 8-12 years; however, not all dogs will fit into that range. Talk to your breeder about the average lifespan of their dogs and what you might expect. Some breeders have had them live over 18 years, but that is definitely the exception rather than the norm.

Most of the health issues are also seen in other breeds, but an illness called Amyloidosis has plagued the breed for many years. It can result in kidney failure and death, starting with high, unexplained fevers at as young as 9-10 weeks old. Their hocks or muzzle tend to swell, but not always. Careful and conscientious breeding can, at best, minimize the chances of offspring suffering from this horrible disease.

Also, eye surgery may be needed due to Entropion (lids rolling in). When puppies are around two weeks of age, they sometimes need "eye tacking" to hold back the excess skin. After a couple of weeks, tacks can be removed in hopes that the puppy has developed enough muscle to hold them open on their own.

Personality and Temperament

An alert and moderately active breed, the Shar-Pei is an independent dog. Although he has a mind of his own, this is a deeply devoted and affectionate breed with his family. With strangers, the dogs are more aloof, to the point of being unfriendly. Like many Asian breeds, the Shar-Pei has strong guard instincts and is an excellent watch dog.

Typically, however, the breed is not aggressive. A Shar-Pei will pin down his adversary and hold him in place, but he will rarely bite. He also retains some of his native hunting instinct, using his good vision and patience to stalk "prey." Vision can sometimes be limited due to framing wrinkles around the eyes. As well as their strong hunting instincts, which include tracking, they also have strong herding instincts.

Shar-Pei love to play with other dogs they have accepted as friends and with their humans. The breed is inventive, fun, and amusing, especially when young. Owners frequently say it's fascinating to watch a Shar-Pei in action, thinking out a plan and diving in when he's made up his mind what to do next.

People don't think that Shar-Pei like to be petted on their head, but actually it is their limited vision from the top of their heads that make them duck when you start to pet them. They have a kind of hood over the top of their eyes. Once they know who is petting them, they love to be petted.

The Shar-Pei Puppy

Having any new puppy in the house means you're dealing with a small dog entertaining visions of grandeur. With a

Shar-Pei, multiply that several times! It's hard to stay too annoyed, or for that matter to even keep a straight face, when you're looking at an adorable little mass of wrinkled mischief. Good preparation in advance will help — that and a complete understanding of the fact that all puppies are work!

This is an important stage in your Shar-Pei's life, and one that demands your active attention and involvement. A dog's adult behavior and temperament are shaped during those first weeks in a new home. It's your responsibility to ensure the dog receives the necessary support and training to be a well-mannered, obedient companion.

Some of the specific tasks you want to accomplish early in your relationship include the following:

- puppy-proofing the house before you bring your pet home
- putting in place the necessary equipment for crate and house training
- deciding how you will manage a healthy diet
- learning the grooming protocol appropriate for the breed
- planning a program of socialization with other dogs and with people

In these opening weeks, you want to get ahead of negative behaviors like jumping, whining, and barking. If you don't have the time to spend working with your dog in the areas that will make him a desirable companion, ask yourself if this is really the time in your life to have a pet. Shar-Pei as a breed are not a "needy" dog, and therefore should not suffer from separation anxiety as long as they are correctly trained.

Also, bear in mind that you are also your dog's companion. This is not a one-sided relationship. What is your work schedule? Do you have to travel often and for extended periods? Be responsible and only adopt one of these dogs if you have time to spend with your pet.

The Need for Socialization

Bad habits can surface in any breed, but it is especially important to ensure that your Shar-Pei puppy is well socialized. Although intensely devoted to their humans, the breed can be standoffish with strangers. They do, however, tend to get along well with other dogs, and even with cats if they have received proper training.

By 10-12 weeks of age you should get your dog into a basic obedience class with a trainer who has experience with the breed. Note that most vets recommend a puppy not be exposed to the company of other dogs until it has received all the required rabies, distemper, and parvovirus vaccinations.

Sending your dog to "school" means that you are enrolled as well. You are there to learn how to be the "leader of the pack." Remember that the Shar-Pei is an intelligent breed known for planning and problem solving. If you don't want to be putty in his paws, do your homework and listen to the trainer!

With Children

The Shar-Pei does very well when raised with kids but I don't think it is a good idea to have ANY dog with children under 3-4 years old. Prior to that they don't understand that pinching, pulling and grabbing is not ok and the dog could bite in self-defense.

Wait until your children are 4-5 years of age, when they are old enough to understand the Shar-Pei's disposition and to respect his boundaries.

Teach children to interact properly with all animals, showing kindness and respect. Don't leave a young child alone with any dog, no matter how good-natured you believe the animal to be. If a child hurts the dog even unintentionally, the dog will react. Don't put either your child or your dog in that position.

Photo Credit: Lauren J Alexander of Lauren's Shar-Pei

With Other Pets

Because Shar-Pei are guard dogs, they can show aggression toward other animals and people. The key to avoiding these problems is a combination of early training and socialization. Your dog will instinctively be wary of strangers and will look to you for signals about who is and is not welcome in your shared "territory."

Issues of aggression can also be circumvented by neutering males. Typically if a Shar-Pei puppy is introduced to other animals early in life, he will see them as part of his family unit as well and interactions will be positive. Shar-Pei do fine with cats if raised with them.

As for other types of pets, exercise reasonable caution. It would not, for instance, be a great idea to let any kind of dog play with a rabbit – and remember that Shar-Pei have been used as hunting dogs. For pets like birds or fish, dogs tend to just ignore them.

Male or Female?

In the vast majority of breeds, gender truly is not an issue in determining personality. The choice only becomes critical if you are considering breeding your dog. For the most part, adoptions should focus on personality and heredity. A dog's genetics and his life experiences exert an enormous influence on his temperament and behavior.

Don't fall for the idea that female dogs are sweeter. It's a groundless assumption, and one that is often wrong, especially with intact individuals experiencing hormonal shifts. Most experts agree that females that have been spoiled and coddled when young show more territoriality than adult males.

The primary reason cited for not wanting a male dog is spraying and urine marking. With a purebred adoption, neutering the dog is a requirement to protect the breeder's bloodlines. The procedures also carry real health benefits. The surgery decreases hormone levels. It puts an end to territorial urine marking in males, and solves the issue of moodiness in females in heat. Beyond these considerations, regard Shar-Pei as basically gender neutral dogs. Pick the healthiest puppy with the best personality and with which you seem to have an instant rapport.

One or Two?

When you are sitting on the floor surrounded by puppies, taking two home seems like a great idea. Pause, take a breath, and think again. Adopting a single dog is a huge commitment. You are pledging your time and money to a living creature.

With the second dog, all of that doubles. Shar-Pei require positive training and socialization to be good pets. They are not dogs for "first timers." If you've never owned the breed before, start slow. You need to really be certain that a Shar-Pei is "the" dog for you before taking on the responsibility of caring for more than one.

Puppy or Adult Dog?

Just look at a cute Shar-Pei puppy and you'll know why people fall for them. The Shar-Pei life expectancy is about 10 years on average, so most people do opt to take in a young dog to have the most amount of time with their pet.

I will say, however, that adopting an adult from a shelter or a rescue situation is a tremendous act of kindness. I wholeheartedly support the lifesaving work of these organizations. There is an appalling epidemic of homeless companion animals in the world.

A Shar-Pei surrendered for adoption will, however, most likely have behavior issues. Find out in advance exactly why the dog was given up. In the best-case scenario, it may simply be an instance of the previous owner no longer being able to care for the dog. If, however, there was a problem, make sure it's one with which you can cope before taking the dog home.

If you don't decide to adopt a dog (of any breed) under rescue circumstances, please support the work of these invaluable organizations with your donations or volunteer hours. These groups are constantly in need and they perform a vital service, literally saving thousands of canine lives each year.

Famous Shar-Pei and Their Owners

The growing popularity of the Shar-Pei has put the dogs more solidly in the public eye. Their responsiveness to taking direction has made the breed naturals for television and motion picture appearances even though they have a well-known reputation for being stubborn and "independent thinkers."

In Great Britain a Shar-Pei is a recognized spokes-"person" for an anti-wrinkle cream (apt product association), while another in New Zealand sells paper towels.

An animated Shar-Pei named Lao Tzu was part of the cast of "The Simpsons," and one named Nikko toured with his owner, Jordan Knight of the band New Kids on the Block. Another Shar-Pei, Bpo Bpo, was part of the cast of the popular series *Lost*.

More recently, in 2013, a Shar-Pei became part of the David Beckham household, and other celebrities have owned the dogs, including: Burt Reynolds, William Shatner, Wayne Newton, Andy Gibb, Ray Liotta, Joanna Carson, the late Yul Brunner, NBA basketball player Carmelo Anthony, and even the King of Morocco.

Photo Credit: Georgette Schaefer of Yu Kou Shar-Pei

Chapter 2 – Shar-Pei Dog Breed Standard

The following information is reproduced verbatim. It is the text of the American Kennel Club's Breed Standard for the Shar-Pei.

Photo Credit: Cate Stewart of Nordic Star Shar-Pei

Official Standard of the Chinese Shar-Pei

General Appearance: An alert, compact dog of medium size and substance; square in profile, close coupled; the well-proportioned head slightly but not overly large for the body. The short, harsh coat, the loose skin covering the head and body, the small ears, the "hippopotamus" muzzle shape and the high set tail impart to the Shar-Pei a unique look peculiar to him alone. The loose skin and wrinkles covering the head, neck and body are superabundant in puppies but these features may be limited to the head, neck and withers in the adult.

Size, Proportion, Substance: The height is 18 to 20 inches at the withers. The weight is 45 to 60 pounds. The dog is usually larger and more square-bodied than the bitch but both appear well proportioned. The height of the Shar-Pei from the ground to the withers is approximately equal to the length from the point of breastbone to the point of rump.

Head and Skull: The *head* is large, slightly, but not overly, proudly carried and covered with profuse wrinkles on the forehead continuing into side wrinkles framing the face.

Eyes - Dark, small, almond-shaped and sunken, displaying a scowling expression. In the dilute-colored dogs the eye color may be lighter.

Ears - extremely small, rather thick, equilateral triangles in shape, slightly rounded at the tips; edges of the ear may curl. Ears lie flat against the head, are set high, wide apart and forward on the skull, pointing toward the eyes. The ears have the ability to move. *A pricked ear is a disqualification.*

Skull - flat and broad, the stop moderately defined.

Muzzle - one of the distinctive features of the breed. It is broad and full with no suggestion of snipiness. (The length from nose to stop is approximately the same as from stop to occiput.)

Nose - large and wide and darkly pigmented, preferably black but any color conforming to the general coat color of the dog is acceptable. In dilute colors, the preferred nose is self-colored. Darkly pigmented cream Shar-Pei may have some light pigment either in the center of the nose or on the entire nose. The lips and top of muzzle are well-padded and may cause a slight bulge above the nose.

Tongue, roof of mouth, gums and flews - solid bluish-black is preferred in all coat colors except in dilute colors, which have a solid lavender pigmentation. A spotted pink tongue is a major fault. *A solid pink tongue is a disqualification.* (Tongue colors may lighten due to heat stress; care must be taken not to confuse dilute pigmentation with a pink tongue.) *Teeth* - strong, meeting in a scissors *bite*. Deviation from a scissors bite is a major fault.

Neck, Topline, Body: *Neck* - medium length, full and set well into the shoulders. There are moderate to heavy folds of loose skin and abundant dewlap about the neck and throat. The *topline* dips slightly behind the withers, slightly rising over the short, broad loin. A level, roach or swayed topline/backline shall be faulted. *Chest* - broad and deep with the brisket extending to the elbow and rising slightly under the loin. *Back* - short and close-coupled. *Croup* - flat, with the base of the tail set extremely high, clearly exposing an up-tilted anus. *Tail* - the high set tail is a characteristic feature of the Shar-Pei. A low set tail shall be faulted. The tail is thick and round at the base, tapering to a fine point and curling over or to either side of the back. *The absence of a complete tail is a disqualification.*

Forequarters: *Shoulders* - muscular, well laid back and sloping. *Forelegs* - when viewed from the front, straight moderately spaced, with elbows close to the body. When viewed from the side, the forelegs are straight, the pasterns are strong and flexible. The bone is substantial but never heavy and is of moderate length. Removal of front dewclaws is optional. *Feet* - moderate in size, compact and firmly set, not splayed.

Hindquarters: Muscular, strong, and moderately angulated. The metatarsi (hocks) are short, perpendicular to the ground and parallel to each other when viewed from the rear. Hind dewclaws must be removed. Feet as in front.

Coat: The extremely harsh coat is one of the distinguishing features of the breed. The coat is absolutely straight and off standing on the main trunk of the body but generally lies somewhat flatter on the limbs. The coat appears healthy without being shiny or lustrous. Acceptable coat lengths may range from extremely short "horse coat" up to the "brush coat," not to exceed 1 inch in length at the withers. A soft coat, a wavy coat, a coat in excess of one inch at the withers or a coat that has been trimmed is a major fault. The Shar-Pei is shown in its natural state.

Color: Only solid colors and sable are acceptable and are to be judged on an equal basis. A solid-color dog may have shading, primarily darker, down the back and on the ears. The shading must be variations of the same body color and may include darker hairs throughout the coat. *The following colors are disqualifications: Albino; not a solid color, i.e.: brindle; parti-colored; spotted; patterned in any combination of colors.*

Gait: The movement of the Shar-Pei is to be judged at a trot. The gait is free and balanced with the feet tending to converge on a center line of gravity when the dog moves at a vigorous trot. The gait combines good forward reach and strong drive in the hindquarters. Proper movement is essential.

Temperament: Regal, alert, intelligent, dignified, lordly, scowling, sober and snobbish essentially independent and somewhat standoffish with strangers, but extreme in his devotion to his family. The Shar-Pei stands firmly on the ground with a calm, confident stature.

Major Faults: *Deviation from a scissors bite. Spotted tongue. A soft coat, a wavy coat, a coat in excess of 1 inch in length at the withers or a coat that has been trimmed.*

Disqualifications: *Pricked ears. Solid pink tongue. Absence of a complete tail. Albino; not a solid color, i.e.: brindle; parti-colored; spotted; patterned in any combination of colors.*

Approved January 12, 1998 - Effective February 28, 1998

Photo Credit: Susanna Björnsson of Brekkukots Shar-Pei

Chapter 3 – Getting Serious About Adoption

If you have progressed past the stage of just considering a Shar-Pei and are ready to adopt, we need to cover a few fundamentals. This is not a breed recommended as a "first dog," but if you choose to ignore that advice, it's even more important that you go into a potential transaction armed with some basic information.

Photo Credit: Barbara LaVere of Tzo Wen Shar-Pei

Is a Shar-Pei Right for You?

Many dog owners make breed selections based on appearance alone and wind up regretting their choice. With Shar-Pei, people fall in love with the wrinkles and are hooked without thoroughly investigating the pros and cons of the breed.

It's a good idea, if possible, to spend some time with a Shar-Pei before making your final decision. Clearly you will be meeting with breeders to discuss your potential adoption, but also consider contacting your local or regional kennel club to talk to Shar-Pei owners. (You can also attend a dog show in your area.)

You are looking for people who will give you their honest opinion about the breed. Never adopt any dog until you've learned as much as possible about what it's really like to live with the breed.

There is quite a lot of misinformation about this breed, which is why you need to educate yourself by talking to experts. One of the most common misconceptions is that the wrinkles can harbor dirt and be a site for potential infections unless cleaned regularly.

Cate Stewart of Nordic Star Shar-Pei says: "This is a rather common fallacy. I have had this breed for 30 years and never have known this to be true. If you need to clean between wrinkles the dog is extremely over wrinkled or has a skin disease or infection. Another fallacy is you need to powder between the wrinkles."

Do You Need a License?

Before you bring your Shar-Pei home, you need to think about whether there are any licensing restrictions in your area. Some countries have strict licensing requirements for the keeping of particular animals.

Even if you are not legally required to have a license for your Shar-Pei, you might still want to consider getting one. Having a license for your dog means that there is an official record of your ownership so, should someone find your dog when he gets lost, that person will be able to find your contact information and reconnect you with him.

There are no federal regulations in the United States regarding the licensing of dogs, but most states do require that dogs be licensed by their owners, otherwise you may be subject to a fine.

Fortunately, dog licenses are inexpensive and fairly easy to obtain – you simply file an application with the state and then renew the license each year. In most cases, licensing a dog costs no more than $25.

Selecting a Puppy

Everyone has their own strategy for selecting a puppy, and the breeder will certainly weigh in on this decision as well. I suggest that you go with the puppy that seems most drawn to you. I generally sit somewhat apart from the litter and wait for one of the dogs to come to me. For each puppy you "meet," consider the following basic evaluation.

Basic Evaluation Tips

As you are interacting with a puppy up for adoption, take the time to conduct the following evaluation. These steps will help you to pick a healthy dog to take home.

- Puppies are often sleepy when you first meet them, but then awaken quickly and become alert, energetic, and even mischievous.

- The dog should feel well-nourished to the touch, with a little fat over the ribs. The overall appearance should be plump, healthy, and rounded.

- Although the Shar-Pei coat is short and rough, it should still appear healthy with no dandruff, bald patches, or greasiness.

- Observe the puppy as it walks and runs. It's normal for little dogs to be wobbly, but there should be no sign of physical impairment like a limp or an odd gait.

- Healthy dogs have clear, bright eyes with no evident discharge in the corners or on the muzzle.

- Hold the puppy close to you and listen to its breathing. The sound should be quiet and steady with no coughing or sneezing. Check the nostrils to make sure they are free of any sign of discharge.

- Examine the area around the puppy's anus and genitals. Ensure there is no encrusted fecal matter or any sign of infection or pus.

- Test the dog's hearing by waiting until it is looking away from you and then clapping your hands. The dog should visibly react to the sound.

- To test visual acuity, roll a ball toward the puppy. The dog should notice the motion and react with accuracy in intercepting or investigating the toy.

Once you feel you can choose a puppy with some degree of confidence, start to work on a short list of breeders. Like most things in the modern world, you will likely turn to the Internet and visit breeder websites. I think it is imperative that you find breeders within driving distance of your home. I am not an advocate of shipping live animals, and you will need to visit the facilities prior to actually taking one of the dogs.

Locating Shar-Pei Breeders

A good place to begin your search for a Shar-Pei in the United States is the Chinese Shar-Pei Club of America at cspca.com. The site includes a breeder directory as well as information on rescue dogs. In the UK, visit The Shar-Pei Club of Great Britain at spcgb.org.

You might also contact your local dog club, or discuss your planned adoption with your vet. Advertisements in local or regional newspapers and magazines are an "iffy" matter at best. Often the dogs listed there are either the product of puppy mills or have been born to "backyard breeders."

Most backyard breeders are perfectly legitimate and well-intentioned people who have simply allowed their pet to breed with another Shar-Pei. It isn't inherently a "bad" situation, but you will receive little if any verifiable information about the dogs.

Also, since most purebred adoptions require that the puppies be spayed or neutered before 6 months of age, you may well not be getting a Shar-Pei. Sometimes the breed is crossed with its near relative the Chow Chow. To the uninitiated, the resulting puppies may well be mistaken for Shar-Pei.

Puppy mills, however, are much more disturbing and exist purely to make a profit. The dogs are generally kept in deplorable conditions with little if any health care and no socialization. You should always be able to see where a puppy was born and evaluate the conditions in which it has been living. If you are not allowed to do so, be suspicious.

Even when you are dealing with breeders online (a ripe ground for puppy mills), modern technology should allow you to videoconference with the breeder, see the entire litter and the parents, and tour the facility.

This kind of "eyes on" evaluation, coupled with discussions with a knowledgeable breeder, is the foundation for a successful adoption. Responsible owners are so enthusiastic about the Shar-Pei you can hardly stop them from talking about their dogs!

Always listen to your gut in dealing with people offering puppies for adoption. If you think something is "off" about the person and the facility, it probably is. Move on! And if you are sufficiently concerned that the dogs are being mistreated or exploited in any way, file a report with animal welfare.

Timing Your Adoption

Timing is more important in adopting a purebred dog than you might think. It is never a good sign when a facility tells you puppies are available year round. That's a definite red flag that you may be talking to a puppy mill.

The normal course of events is that you make contact with the breeder and your name is put on a waiting list. You may even be asked to place a small deposit to reserve a dog from a future litter. Generally if you decide not to adopt, the amount is refunded. Don't just assume this is the case, however. Always ask for details of any transaction.

Breeders are so protective about the health of their females that litters are only born twice per year, usually in the spring and summer. Scheduling births for the warmer months allows more time to work with the dogs outdoors, which increases opportunities for socialization in a variety of settings.

You should also think about timing in regard to your own life. If you are involved in a major project at work or it's the holidays, bringing a puppy into the chaos may not be the best idea. Dogs are creatures of habit. They need routine to help them start a new life and learn to be reliable companions.

Approximate Purchase Price

Prices vary widely, but pet-quality Shar-Pei puppies from reputable breeders are typically offered in a price range of $500 to $2,000+ / £350 to £1,282+. A show-quality puppy starts at $1,000 / £650 and up.

These websites can be good places to begin your search:

Adopt a Pet — http://www.adoptapet.com
Petango — http://www.petango.com
Pei People – http://www.peipeople.com (They rescue from the states of California, Arizona and Nevada).
Puppy Find — http://www.puppyfind.com/
Oodle - http://dogs.oodle.com/

Pros and Cons of Owning a Shar-Pei

Discussing the pros and cons of a breed draws me up short. I don't see the question as one that can be answered definitively. What one person loves about a breed might well drive another to the brink of insanity. Take the Jack Russell, for instance. It's a fantastically smart breed with the will of a Marine drill sergeant. This breed transcends the idea of alpha. I think they're great dogs, but I don't want to live with one!

A Shar-Pei breeder should always be willing to discuss the positive and negatives of the breed and should try to help you decide if the breed is a good fit in your life. The one overriding concern should always be the welfare of the dogs. Shar-Pei are exceptional dogs and they deserve exceptional homes.

Reasons to Adopt a Shar-Pei

- Easy to housebreak and clean by nature
- Minimal shedding
- Require little grooming
- Natural guard dog
- Affectionate and devoted with their family
- Incredibly smart and intuitive
- Get along well with other pets under the right circumstances

Reasons NOT to Adopt a Shar-Pei

- Not a breed for first-time dog owners
- Stubborn, independent, and difficult to train
- Require extensive socialization; aloof with strangers
- Prone to yeast skin infections (mainly from ears and between toes)
- Territorial and often overly possessive of their owners
- Can develop aggression issues with other dogs
- Prone to kidney disease and other genetic issues
- They are incredibly smart and will learn bad habits very quickly. It is difficult to break the bad habits, especially if they involve food. They get bored easily and once they know a behavior, they are eager to go on to the next thing.

Chapter 4 – Buying a Shar-Pei

If this will be your first pedigreed adoption, there may be aspects of the process for which you are not prepared. The following information should cover the highlights of the associated procedures and help you to understand why breeders require certain things from their clients.

Photo Credit: Cate Stewart of Nordic Star Shar-Pei

Pet Quality vs. Show Quality

In the world of purebred dogs, puppies are rated as either pet quality or show quality. Prices reflect this delineation, but the practice illustrates the dedication with which breeders work to improve their bloodlines.

Puppies that are not considered to be superior examples of the Shar-Pei breed are classed as "pet quality" and offered for sale to good homes. Even when the owner points out these so-called "flaws," you will likely see nothing "wrong" with the

cute and lively little dog that is about to become your best
friend.

Show-quality dogs are much more expensive and are headed
both for competitive exhibition and a role in breeding
programs. If you do buy a show-quality dog, you do so out of
a desire to either exhibit the animal or to become a breeder
yourself, topics that will be covered later in this book.

Bobbie Libman of Mikobi Shar-Pei advises as follows: "When
determining 'pet' or 'show' quality, it is usually done at
around 8-10 weeks of age. The best time to buy a 'show' pup
would best be when the pup has reached 6 months of age.
However, most breeders do not want to keep the litter for that
long a time. The permanent teeth come in around 4 months
old, so the proper 'bite' can be assessed. Also, when they
grow, their movement can change as well. When I evaluate a
young puppy, I categorize it as having 'show potential.' I do
not give a guarantee that they are going to stay together and I
do not replace a dog if it doesn't turn out. Long-time breeders
are best at hazarding an 'educated guess' to determine the
future the pup will have in the show ring."

Spaying and Neutering Required

When you buy a pet-quality pedigree puppy the standard
purchase agreement requires the animal to be spayed or
neutered before six months of age. Again, this is tied to the
goal of improving the breed.

Pet-quality puppies are not qualified to be used in breeding
programs and the stipulation is to ensure their "flaws" are not
passed on. This requirement also helps to ensure that the dogs
do not wind up at the mercy of unscrupulous puppy mills.

Choosing a Breeder

Always work with a local or regional breeder so that you can pick up your dog in person. I do not support shipping animals unless it is an absolute necessity, and never in the cargo hold of the plane. There are too many things that can and do go wrong. Subjecting a young animal to the hazards of travel is simply not, in my opinion, a good decision.

Even if you do find your Shar-Pei online, visiting the breeder in person at least once is essential. You need to assess not only the condition of the facility, but the behavior of the breeder. Any breeder that is unwilling to agree to such a visit should be regarded with suspicion.

At a kennel or home, you should always be allowed to see the entire litter and, if possible, to meet both parents. In talking with the breeder, you should have the sense of information flowing freely in both directions with no guarded or vague tone to the exchange.

Nowadays many breeders are home based and their dogs live in the house as pets. Puppies are typically raised in the breeder's home as well. It's very common for Shar-Pei breeders to use guardian homes for their breeding dogs. A guardian home is a permanent family for the dog. The breeder retains ownership of the dog during the years the dog is used for breeding, but the dog lives with the guardian family. This arrangement is great for the dog because once retired from breeding he/she is spayed/neutered and returned to its forever family. There is no need to re-home the dog after its breeding career has ended. There are still breeders who use kennels, but the number of home breeders is quite high.

Expectations with a Good Breeder

Good breeders help you pick your puppy. Their goal is to place the dog in a good home. Above all else, the future welfare of the animal should be front and center in the conversation. The following are all signs that you are working with a good breeder.

- You are allowed to see all the puppies with the mother and to meet the father if he is in residence at the breeder. These interactions will give you some chance to judge the temperament of the adult dogs and a sense of the eventual size and conformation of the puppies.

- You are allowed to handle all the puppies rather than being presented with a single dog available for adoption.

- Breeders of purebred dogs register litters with the governing kennel club and select an official name for each dog. The puppies are registered in the breeder's name until they go to new homes, at which time the registration is transferred into the name of the new owners. This process should be explained to you in full.

- You are given a complete description of how the puppy has been socialized along with advice on successfully continuing the process at home.

Questions You Must Answer

Breeders want to know their dogs are going to good homes. You will be asked questions about such things as your home, work schedule, family, and other pets. This is not prying into your life. It is an excellent sign that you are working with a professional with a genuine interest in placing their dogs appropriately.

You want the breeder to be a resource for you in the future if you need help or guidance in living with your Shar-Pei. Be receptive to answering your breeder's queries and open to having an ongoing friendship.

It is quite common for breeders to call and check on how their dogs are doing and to make themselves available to answer questions.

What the Breeder Should Provide to You

All of the following items should be provided to you as part of the adoption process and you should receive complete answers to all questions you have regarding any of these provisions or others included in the transaction.

- **Contract of sale.** This document should detail the responsibilities of both parties and explain the transfer of the registration papers.

- **Information packet.** This material should include advice on feeding, training and exercise as well as health procedures like worming and vaccinations.

- **Pedigree**. This is a record of the dog's ancestry either in handwriting or an official copy from the governing kennel club.

- **All health records.** You should be given copies of all health records for the puppy (and parents), in particular the schedule of vaccinations and required boosters. Full disclosure of any potential genetic conditions associated with the breed should accompany these records as well as the results of any testing or screening performed. Note that while screening or testing obviously helps reduce risks, there can never be a complete guarantee that problems will not occur.

- **Health guarantee.** The guarantee confirms the health of the puppy at the time of the adoption with a stipulation that this fact be confirmed with a vet within a specified time period. There should also be a detailed explanation of recompense in the event that a health condition does arise within the length of the guarantee.

Photo Credit: Lynn and Michael Olds of Lava Kennels

Identification Systems for Pedigree Dogs

Pedigreed dogs may or may not have a means of permanent identification on their bodies when they are adopted. Governing organizations use differing systems. The American Kennel Club recommends permanent identification as a "common sense" practice. The preferred options are tattoos or microchips.

In the United Kingdom, the Kennel Club is the only organization accredited by the United Kingdom Accreditation Service to certify dog breeders through the Kennel Club Assured Breeder Scheme. Under this program, breeders must permanently identify their breeding stock by microchip, tattoo, or DNA profile.

Any dogs traveling to or returning to the UK from another country can do so under the Pet Passport system, for which microchipping is a requirement. For more information see www.gov.uk/take-pet-abroad. All dogs registered with the Canadian Kennel Club must be permanently identified with either a tattoo or a microchip.

Warning Signs of a Bad Breeder

Each of the following scenarios indicates you may be working with a bad breeder. Do not gloss over any of these "red flags."

- Being told there is no need for you to come to the breeder's home or kennel in person.

- Assurances that buying a puppy, sight unseen, is normal.

- Refusal to allow clients to see where the dogs are currently living.

- Overcrowded conditions in which the dogs are apprehensive and nervous around people.

- No access to meet either of the puppy's parents and no access to verifiable information about them.

- No medical records for the dogs or promises the records will be sent "later."

- Failure to provide a health guarantee.

- No signed bill of sale or promises that one will be forwarded.

Beware of "breeders" who tell you they have rare colors with names not noted in the standard. These color breeders are usually backyard breeders in it to sell "rare color dogs" for extortionate amounts.

Avoiding Scam Puppy Sales

Puppy mills exist only to produce the maximum number of dogs at minimal expense for the greatest profit. The dogs are raised in substandard and often horrific conditions. There is no concern for their health or consideration of the effects of environment on their adult behavior. Inbreeding is common, leading to genetic issues and short lifespan.

In order to help fight the proliferation of these deplorable operations, avoid pet shops and beware of online scams! Both venues are prime outlets for dogs raised in puppy mills. If you cannot afford a pedigreed dog, adopt from a shelter or a rescue group. These entities have the best interests of the animals at heart and are often desperately trying to place dogs that would otherwise be euthanized.

Some scammers will advertise a single puppy on the free-to-advertise websites and get you to pay a "deposit" over the

Internet. They leave the advert open long enough to rake in a number of deposits then remove the ad and create a new one from a different location.

Unfortunately, the Internet is full of these kinds of operations, as are many pet stores. If you don't have the money to work with a breeder, think about a shelter or rescue adoption, even if you can't be certain of adopting a Shar-Pei. You CAN be certain you will be helping an animal in need and saving a life.

Best Age to Purchase a Shar-Pei Puppy

A Shar-Pei puppy needs time to learn important life skills from the mother dog, including eating solid food and grooming themselves.

For the first month of a puppy's life, they will be on a mother's milk-only diet. Once the puppy's teeth begin to appear, they will start to be weaned from mother's milk, and by the age of 8 weeks should be completely weaned and eating just puppy food.

Puppies generally leave between 10-12 weeks and are usually weaned before they receive their first vaccines. It is not beneficial for the pup to stay longer, as it can have a negative affect for several reasons. One is that the puppy should not have access to nursing after their first vaccine, otherwise that vaccine is void. Some moms will continue to nurse despite the puppy being on solid food.

In other cases, the mom is too overwhelmed with the size of the pups and the size of the litter and she avoids them. This occurs as early as 6 weeks old and can result in bad behaviors as the puppies interact with each other. Their roughhouse playing becomes more and more imprinted on them, and families could struggle to teach the puppy not to play with children as they do with their litter mates.

Trainers would even highly recommend training and bonding begin with their new families by 8-10 weeks. In addition, pups need to be highly socialized between 8-12 weeks with new people, new experiences and places. This time period is very crucial in developing a well-rounded pup.

How to Choose a Puppy?

My best advice is to go with the puppy that is drawn to you. My standard strategy in selecting a pup has always been to sit a little apart from a litter and let one of the dogs come to me. My late father was, in his own way, a "dog whisperer." He taught me this trick for picking puppies and it's never let me down.

I've had dogs in my life since childhood and enjoyed a special connection with them all. I will say that often the dog that comes to me isn't the one I might have chosen — but I still consistently rely on this method.

Cate Stewart of Nordic Star Shar-Pei says: "Although this method is ideal, it is not usually how it is done with show breeders. If it is a litter of 5, maybe 3 are available as a pet. The one that comes to you first may not be available to you. Most reputable breeders have waiting lists for puppies, so getting your choice often isn't the case."

You will want to choose a puppy with a friendly, easy-going temperament, and your breeder should be able to help you with your selection. Also ask the breeder about the temperament and personalities of the puppy's parents and if they have socialized the puppies.

Always be certain to ask if a Shar-Pei puppy you are interested in has displayed any signs of aggression or fear, because if this is happening at such an early age, you may experience behavioral troubles as the puppy becomes older.

Beyond this, I suggest that you interact with your dog with a clear understanding that each one is an individual with unique traits. It is not so much a matter of learning about all Shar-Pei, but rather of learning about YOUR Shar-Pei dog.

Checking Puppy Social Skills

When choosing a puppy out of a litter, look for one that is friendly and outgoing, rather than one who is overly aggressive or fearful. Puppies who demonstrate good social skills with their litter mates are much more likely to develop into easy-going, happy adult dogs that play well with others.

Observe all the puppies together and take notice:

Which puppies are comfortable both on top and on the bottom when play fighting and wrestling with their litter mates, and which puppies seem to only like being on top?

Which puppies try to keep the toys away from the other puppies, and which puppies share?

Which puppies seem to like the company of their litter mates, and which ones seem to be loners?

Puppies that ease up or stop rough play when another puppy yelps or cries are more likely to respond appropriately when they play too roughly as adults.

Is the puppy sociable with humans? If they will not come to you, or display fear toward strangers, this could develop into a problem later in their life.

Is the puppy relaxed about being handled? If they are not, they may become difficult with adults and children during daily interactions, grooming or visits to the veterinarian's office.

Check Puppy's Health

Ask to see veterinarian reports to satisfy yourself that the puppy is as healthy as possible. Before making your final pick of the litter, check for general signs of good health, including the following:

1.   Breathing: will be quiet, without coughing or sneezing, and there will be no crusting or discharge around their nostrils.
2.   Body: will look round and well fed, with an obvious layer of fat over their rib cage.
3.   Coat: will be soft with no dandruff or bald spots.
4.   Energy: a well-rested puppy should be alert and energetic.
5.   Hearing: a puppy should react if you clap your hands behind their head.
6.   Genitals: no discharge visible in or around their genital or anal region.
7.   Mobility: they will walk and run normally without wobbling, limping or seeming to be stiff or sore.
8.   Vision: bright, clear eyes with no crust or discharge.

Chapter 5 – Caring for Your Shar-Pei Puppy

There is one undeniable truth about all puppies of all breeds. No matter their size, a puppy can get into big trouble fast. Shar-Pei puppies are no exception. Before you even think about bringing your new dog home, you must "puppy proof" the house.

It's best to think of your new puppy as a super intelligent four-legged toddler. Their minds are as bright and inventive as that of any child, but it comes with a set of teeth bent on destruction and mayhem. Every single thing in your home that can be sniffed, chewed, swallowed, or some combination thereof is free game and therefore in danger.

Household Poisons

Shar-Pei will eat almost anything, especially when they're puppies. A young dog just gulps down whatever is in his path with no forethought, putting him at serious risk for accidental poisoning.

Thoroughly examine any area in the home to which the dog will have access or into which he could gain access. Take away any potential poisons, or get them high up and out of the dog's reach. The better option is really to take them out to the garage or to another outbuilding. You want to be particularly vigilant about:

- cleaning products
- insecticides
- mothballs
- fertilizers
- antifreeze

When in doubt, get it out. Caution is always the best policy. If you don't know whether an item is poisonous, assume that it is. Your puppy should not have access to any type of chemical whatsoever.

Look Around with the Eyes of a Puppy

Puppies investigate everything! Nothing escapes their attention. To really protect your new "baby," get down on the floor at his eye level. When you see things from his perspective, all kinds of hazards you never dreamed existed in your home become evident.

- Look for anything that dangles: drapery pulls, electrical cords, frayed threads on upholstery, or loose wallpaper. Remove or contain those items in some way. Cord minders are a good solution.

- Locate "lost" items that have found their way under your furniture or have become wedged between the furniture cushions. All of these items can be choking hazards. The fact that they are "hidden" and have to be "dug up" will make them all the more enticing.

- Spot "topple" dangers. Puppies love to play tug of war. That's fine if you're on the other end of the rope, but if the "opponent" is the television tethered to a coaxial cable, the whole unit can easily come crashing down.

- Prepare for the chewing. Young dogs will gnaw on anything. Remove all the stuffed items, including sofa pillows, and wrap the legs of prized furniture to protect them.

Anything that could even remotely look like a toy should be taken out of the room. Think I'm exaggerating? Go to your favorite search engine online and type in "dog chewed cell phone." You won't believe what a determined puppy can do!

Plant Dangers, Inside and Out

Both indoor and outdoor plants present a risk, but the list is far longer than most people realize. There's a fair degree of awareness that peach and apricot pits are potentially poisonous, but so are spinach leaves and tomato vines.

The American Society for the Prevention of Cruelty to Animals has created a large reference list of plants for dog owners here.

http://www.aspca.org/pet-care/animal-poison-control/toxic-and-non-toxic-plants

Even the plants that are not potentially lethal can cause severe and painful gastrointestinal upset. It's a myth that dogs will leave houseplants alone. When I say puppies will chew anything, I mean anything — including your plants.

Preparing for the Homecoming

Buy two crates before your puppy's arrival: a travel crate and a wire crate for use in the home. The crate will be an important part of your dog's housebreaking lessons and it's also the best tool to prevent separation anxiety.

Do not make the mistake of buying a huge crate for a little dog. Yes, the puppy may "grow into it," but you'll set back your pet's progress with housebreaking, which, thankfully, seems to be an easy lesson for Shar-Pei to absorb.

The crate theory is simple: an animal will not soil its den. Give a puppy a huge crate, and he will designate one corner as the "bathroom." Don't do anything to confuse a young dog about where it can and can't eliminate.

Base your choice of crates by the size of dog in terms of weight. Ultimately, your Shar-Pei will weigh about 40-60 lbs. on average with a height at the withers of at least 18-20 inches and will need an adult crate that measures:

- 36" X 25" X 27" / 91.44 cm x 63.5 cm x 68.58 cm.

(Note that some larger individuals can weigh as much as 60 lbs. / 27.21 kg.)

Ask your breeder for the puppy's current weight and buy the correct size crate, understanding that you will have to upgrade once, and perhaps twice before an adult crate is appropriate. Trust me, this expense is completely justified.

In addition to a travel crate for the ride home, get a couple of puppy-safe chew toys. Put those items inside the crate with some piece of clothing you've worn recently. This will help your new pet to learn your scent and to begin to see you as the leader of his "pack." Don't forget to secure the crate in place with the seatbelt.

Photo Credit: Susanna Björnsson of Brekkukots Shar-Pei

Ask the breeder to schedule a time for you to pick up your dog in between regular meals. You don't want the puppy getting sick on the ride home. Be sure to take the dog to do his "business" before he gets in the car and again as soon as you arrive home. Always praise a puppy for going in the right spot at the right time.

The ride home will include a lot of whining and crying, which you need to resist. If you don't, you're very smart new pet will immediately peg you for the pushover you are and begin training you to answer his every whim. Beyond any other consideration, a small dog is much safer in a crate in a moving vehicle than riding on someone's lap.

Ask a friend to go with you and ride in the back seat with the puppy (in the crate). Sometimes just a comforting presence is all it takes for a little dog to settle down and go right to sleep.

The transition from the breeder's place to your home should be low key. Don't overwhelm the puppy. If you have children, explain that the trip home needs to be quiet and calm since the puppy is leaving its mother and siblings for the first time. Ask your kids to stay at home, and to be patient about allowing the little dog to settle into his new home.

Take the puppy to the area of the house that has been puppy proofed and let him explore. At the same time you don't want to overload the dog's senses, you also don't want him to feel isolated and nervous. Resist the urge to pick him up every time he cries.

Follow the feeding schedule to which the dog has become accustomed at the breeder's. Routines comfort dogs and give them a sense of safety. Often, breeders will provide a small supply of whatever food the puppy is used to eating.

Continue to use articles of worn clothing to reassure and comfort the puppy and consider leaving a radio playing on low at night so the little dog doesn't feel so alone. A warm water bottle wrapped in soft cloth can also help.

If you bring the puppy to bed with you, be prepared to have your pet there for life. If you want a dog that will sleep through the night in its crate, ignore the pitiful whining.

The Importance of the Crate

Non-dog people have a real misconception about the importance of and role of the crate in a dog's life. The crate isn't the canine version of "jail." In fact, it's the exact opposite. A dog sees its crate as a quiet, safe place — a den. Often a dog that is crate trained will go inside "his space" just to have some alone time.

The crate helps to control separation anxiety, which can be a problem with the Shar-Pei, and makes it easier to travel with your pet. You do not want to ever create negative associations with the crate in your dog's mind. Never put the dog inside because you are frustrated and angry. Do not use the crate as punishment.

Leave the door open and let the dog have the freedom to come and go, praising your dog when he goes inside. Begin closing the door for short periods until he is completely accustomed to the idea that sometimes he will be inside his den until you return. When a dog really understands the role of the crate in his life, the arrangement gives him and you much greater peace of mind.

Slow Introductions with the Children

For the safety and comfort of all concerned, supervise your children's interactions with the new puppy. Children must be taught to handle all animals safely and with kindness.

Don't let the kids wear the puppy out during its first day or two at home. Let the dog have time to adjust. Shar-Pei have a reputation for being tolerant with children, but the breed doesn't like to be cuddled or held.

What Can I Do to Make My Shar-Pei Love Me?

From the moment you bring your Shar-Pei dog home, every minute you spend with him is an opportunity to bond. The earlier you start working with your dog, the more quickly that bond will grow and the closer you and your Shar-Pei will become.

While simply spending time with your Shar-Pei will encourage the growth of that bond, there are a few things you can do to purposefully build your bond with your dog. Some of these things include:

•   Taking your Shar-Pei for daily walks during which you frequently stop to pet and talk to your dog.

•   Engaging your Shar-Pei in games like fetch and hide-and-seek to encourage interaction.

•   Interact with your dog through daily training sessions – teach your dog to pay attention when you say his name.

•   Be calm and consistent when training your dog – always use positive reinforcement rather than punishment.

•   Spend as much time with your Shar-Pei as possible, even if it means simply keeping the dog in the room with you while you cook dinner or pay bills.

Common Mistakes to Avoid

Never pick your Shar-Pei puppy up if they are showing fear or aggression toward an object, another dog or person, because this will be rewarding them for unbalanced behavior.

If they are doing something you do not want them to continue, your puppy needs to be gently corrected by you with firm and calm energy, so that they learn not to react with fear or aggression. When the mum of the litter tells her puppies off, she will use a deep noise with strong eye contact, until the puppy quickly realizes it's doing something naughty.

Don't play the "hand" game, where you slide the puppy across the floor with your hands, because it's amusing for humans to see a little ball of fur scrambling to collect themselves and run back across the floor for another go.

This sort of "game" will teach your puppy to disrespect you as their leader in two different ways — first, because this "game" teaches them that humans are their play toys, and secondly, this type of "game" teaches them that humans are a source of excitement.

When your Shar-Pei puppy is teething, they will naturally want to chew on everything within reach, and this will include you. As cute as you might think it is when they are young puppies, this is not an acceptable behavior, and you need to gently, but firmly, discourage the habit, just like a mother dog does to her puppies when they need to be weaned.

Always praise your puppy when they stop inappropriate behavior, as this is the beginning of teaching them to understand rules and boundaries. Often we humans are quick to discipline a puppy or dog for inappropriate behavior, but we forget to praise them for their good behavior.

Don't treat your Shar-Pei like a small, furry human. When people try to turn dogs into people, this can cause them much stress and confusion that could lead to behavioral problems.

A well-behaved Shar-Pei thrives on rules and boundaries, and when they understand that there is no question you are their leader and they are your follower, they will live a contented, happy and stress-free life.

Dogs are a different species with different rules; for example, they do not naturally cuddle, and they need to learn to be stroked and cuddled by humans. Therefore, be careful when approaching a dog for the first time and being overly expressive with your hands. The safest areas to touch are the back and chest — avoid patting on the head and touching the ears.

Many people will assume that a dog that is yawning is tired — this is often a misinterpretation, and instead it is signaling your dog is uncomfortable and nervous about a situation.

Be careful when staring at dogs because this is one of the ways in which they threaten each other. This body language can make them feel distinctly uneasy.

Introductions with Other Pets

Although Shar-Pei were once fighting dogs, they have a reputation for getting along moderately well with other animals in the family. The most tentative first meeting will likely be with the family cat.

Because I know Shar-Pei that live in peace with other animals, I'm offering you the complete range of conventional wisdom in regard to this aspect of Shar-Pei ownership. That being said, I would not personally keep a Shar-Pei and a cat.

This is mainly because I am also a great lover of cats and could never live with myself if I created a situation where I placed a living creature in danger by bringing it into my home with a potentially aggressive dog.

The greatest trouble with introductions is more apt to occur when you are bringing animals into a home with an adult

Shar-Pei. You stand a greater chance of success introducing a puppy into a home with existing pets.

Older dogs have ways of putting puppies in their place, usually with a warning growl or bared teeth. This "instructional" behavior isn't something you typically need to worry about. If there are older dogs in the house, make sure they are still getting enough of your attention and allow the hierarchy of the pack to assert itself.

For cats already in residence, the tried and true method of arranging an introduction with a puppy is under a closed bathroom door. This lets the cat sniff the dog and get used to its scent without having to deal with offensive, in-your-whiskers puppy exuberance. The primary problem cats have with dogs is they are just too effusive and have no respect for feline personal space.

When it comes time for the first face-to-face, don't overreact. If you're upset and nervous, your pets will pick up on your feelings. That added tension doesn't help the situation. If there is an altercation, don't yell. Just separate the animal and try again another day.

Truth be told, when a puppy meets a fully "weaponized" house cat, the chances are far greater that the little dog is the one that will be sent running away yelping. Again, so long as there's no real harm being inflicted on either party, be quiet, issue a firm "no" complete with disapproving glare, and let the animals sort it out for themselves.

While this might not work with all breeds, Shar-Pei are highly intelligent, and learn quickly. The cat may not ever love the dog, but an overall state of detente will be created over time. Cats have a tremendous capacity to ignore people, creatures, and things they do not like.

In a first meeting with another dog, it's generally a good idea to have two people in the room just in case the animals have to be quickly separated and removed to different areas. Your manner always sets the tone, so if you're calm, friendly, and happy, chances are the dogs will be as well.

Puppies most often run into trouble with their elders because they don't understand the etiquette adult dogs use not to overstep territorial bounds. Let the older dog teach those lessons, but do exercise caution at mealtimes. Perceived competition for food can lead to nasty aggressive spats. It's best that all dogs (and cats) have their own bowls and preferably their own place to eat in peace.

Habituation and Socialization

Habituation is when you continuously provide exposure to the same stimuli over a period of time. This will help your Shar-Pei to relax in his environment and will teach him how to behave around unfamiliar people, noises, other pets and different surroundings. Expose your Shar-Pei puppy continuously to new sounds and new environments.

When you allow for your Shar-Pei to face life's positive experiences through socialization and habituation, you're helping your Shar-Pei to build a library of valuable information that he can use when he's faced with a difficult situation. If he's had plenty of wonderful and positive early experiences, the more likely he'll be able to bounce back from any surprising or scary experiences.

When your Shar-Pei puppy arrives at his new home for the first time, he'll start bonding with his human family immediately. This will be his primary bond. His secondary bond will be with everyone outside your home. A dog should never be secluded inside his home. Be sure to find the right balance where you're not exposing your Shar-Pei puppy to too much external stimuli. If he starts becoming fearful, speak to your veterinarian.

The puppyhood journey can be tiresome yet very rewarding. Primary socialization starts between three and five weeks of age, where a pup's experiences take place within his litter. This will have a huge impact on all his future emotional behavior.

Socialization from six to twelve weeks allows for puppies to bond with other species outside of their littermates and parents. It's at this particular stage that most pet parents will bring home a puppy and where he'll soon become comfortable with humans, other pets and children.

By the time a puppy is around twelve to fourteen weeks, he becomes more difficult to introduce to new environments and new people and starts showing suspicion and distress.

Nonetheless, if you've recently adopted a Shar-Pei puppy or are bringing one home and he's beyond this ideal age, don't neglect to continue the socialization process. Puppies need to be exposed to as many new situations, environments, people and other animals as possible, and it is never too late to start.

During puppyhood, you can easily teach your puppy to politely greet a new person, yet by the time a puppy has reached social maturity, the same puppy, if not properly socialized, may start lunging forward and acting aggressively, with the final outcome of lunging and nipping.

Never accidentally reward your Shar-Pei puppy for displaying fear or growling at another dog or animal by picking them up. Picking up a Shar-Pei puppy or dog at this time, when they are displaying unbalanced energy, actually turns out to be a reward for them, and you will be teaching them to continue with this type of behavior. As well, picking up a puppy literally places them in a "top dog" position where they are higher and more dominant than the dog or animal they just growled at.

The correct action to take in such a situation is to gently correct your puppy with a firm yet calm energy by distracting them with a "No," so that they learn to let you deal with the situation on their behalf.

If you allow a fearful or nervous puppy to deal with situations that unnerve them all by themselves, they may learn to react with fear or aggression, and you will have created a problem that could escalate into something quite serious as they grow older.

The same is true of situations where a young puppy may feel the need to protect themselves from a bigger or older dog that may come charging in for a sniff. It is the guardian's responsibility to protect the puppy so that they do not think they must react with fear or aggression in order to protect themselves.

Once your Shar-Pei puppy has received all their vaccinations, you can take them out to public dog parks and various locations where many dogs are found.

Before allowing them to interact with other dogs or puppies, take them for a disciplined walk on leash so that they will be a little tired and less likely to immediately engage with all other dogs.

Keep your puppy on leash and close beside you, because most puppies are usually a bundle of out-of-control energy, and you need to protect them while teaching them how far they can go before getting themselves into trouble with adult dogs who may not appreciate excited puppy playfulness.

If your puppy shows any signs of aggression or domination toward another dog, you must immediately step in and calmly discipline them.

Take your puppy everywhere with you and introduce them to many different people of all ages, sizes and ethnicities. Most people will come to you and want to interact with your puppy. If they ask if they can hold your puppy, let them, because so long as they are gentle and don't drop the puppy, this is a good way to socialize your Shar-Pei and show them that humans are friendly.

As important as socialization is, it is also important that the dog be left alone for short periods when young so that they can cope with some periods of isolation. If an owner goes out and they have never experienced this, they can destroy things or make a mess because of panic. They are thinking they are vulnerable and can be attacked by something or someone coming into the house.

Dogs that have been socialized are able to easily diffuse a potentially troublesome situation and hence they will rarely get into fights. Dogs that are poorly socialized often misinterpret or do not understand the subtle signals of other dogs, getting into trouble as a result.

Creating a Safe Environment

Never think for a minute that your Shar-Pei would not bolt and run away. Even well-adjusted, happy puppies and adult dogs can run away, usually in extreme conditions such as with fireworks, thunder or when scared.

Collar, tag and microchip your new Shar-Pei. Microchipping is not enough, since many pet parents tend to presume that dogs without collars are homeless or have been abandoned.

Recent photos of your Shar-Pei with the latest clip need to be placed in your wallet or purse.

Train your Shar-Pei – foster and work with a professional, positive trainer to ensure that your Shar-Pei does not run out the front door or out the backyard gate. Teach your Shar-Pei basic, simple commands such as "come" and "stay."

Create a special, fun digging area just for him; hide his bones and toys and let your Shar-Pei know that it's okay to dig in that area. After all, dogs need to play!

Introduce your new, furry companion to all your neighbors so everyone will know that he belongs to you.

Puppy Nutrition

The most successful nutritional programs for dogs are those that track your pet's growth. Puppies aged four months and under need four meals per day. That can be reduced to three feedings in months 4-8, and then two feedings for life, morning and evening.

Your puppy's feeding schedule is an addendum to his housebreaking. Don't "free feed" a young dog, which is the practice of having dry food out at all times. This may work for an adult if weight gain is not an issue, but regular feeding times for a puppy set the pattern for trips outside.

Put the food down and leave it for 10-20 minutes, then take it up — even if your dog hasn't "finished." You are not depriving your pet, but instead getting him accustomed to a routine that will help you both.

Rely on premium, high-quality dry food. Your best option is to give your Shar-Pei whatever it's been eating at the breeder's. If you want to transition your pet to a different product, the change should only occur slowly and over time. Sudden dietary changes throw puppies into major gastrointestinal upset.

To make an effective food transition, mix the existing diet with the new food, slowly changing the percentage of new to old over a period of 10 days.

The vast majority of breeders recommend not feeding puppy food. It can be high in protein and actually can cause the puppy to grow too fast, thus possibly creating bone growth issues.

Always read the label on any food you are using. The first ingredients listed should be meat or fishmeal. High percentages of meat by-products and cornmeal indicate a food with low nutritional value. It will fill your pet up and increase his production of waste, but do little to provide the required vitamins and minerals.

Grain-free is often recommended in the Shar-Pei. Many are allergic to corn, wheat and some other grains. Also no "soy" in the dog food – it irritates them!

Puppies should not receive wet food. It is too rich for their digestion, lacks the correct nutritional balance, and is harder to measure. Portion control is crucial with young dogs. A puppy should only receive the amount of food that is right for his age and weight, information that should be provided on the label of the dog food sack.

Some breeders differ on food advice. Bobbie Libman of Mikobi Shar-Pei does it this way: "I begin feeding solid food at the age of 3 weeks by soaking the kibble and using freeze-dried raw on top with an oatmeal type consistency. I always feed the same food their mother is getting and never feed puppy food to Shar-Pei. It is too high in protein and when they would graduate to a different diet, sometimes it could cause digestion issues. My pups have always done well on the adult food and there is no need to transition when they get more teeth. Puppies are fed 3 times daily until I notice they are not eating as much at their noon meal. I then eliminate the noon meal and I continue feeding twice a day for the rest of their lives. I always feed dogs from stainless steel 2-quart bowls on raised feeding stands."

To avoid messy "tip overs," use weighted stainless steel food and water bowls. Plastic retains odors and breeds bacteria. Bowls in elevated stands create a better posture for the dog while eating – just make sure the arrangement is not too tall for the puppy to reach.

Stainless steel bowl sets sell for less than $25 / £14.87. (Those with an included stand may be priced slightly higher.)

Adult Nutrition

The same basic principles should guide your management of an adult Shar-Pei diet. Pick a product line that offers a graduated program of nutrition from a puppy formula through an adult mix, and finally a senior blend. This creates the perfect arrangement for consistent nutrition for life with seamless transitions from one food to the next.

All dogs are accomplished beggars, they can get hooked on almost anything. Don't let this unhealthy dietary habit get started! Even when you give your dog proper canine treats, those items should never constitute more than 5% of the total daily food intake. This caution is not just in reference to weight gain. Many human foods are toxic to dogs, including, but not limited to:

- Chocolate
- Raisins
- Alcohol
- Human vitamins (especially those with iron)
- Mushrooms
- Onions and garlic
- Walnuts
- Macadamia nuts
- Raw fish

- Raw pork
- Raw chicken

Any bones given to a puppy should be too large to swallow. Bones are both a choke and "splinter" hazard. The sharp pieces can lacerate the throat and intestines. Supervise a dog chewing on a bone and take the item away at the first sign of splintering.

There is an idea that a dog "should" be given animal bones. I am against this practice. There are excellent "puppy-safe" chew products that are also beneficial to keep your pet's teeth clean and in good shape. These commercial products are a much better and safer option.

The Canine Teeth and Jaw

Even today, far too many dog food choices continue to have far more to do with being convenient for us humans to serve, than they do with being a well-balanced, healthy food choice.

In order to choose the right food for your Shar-Pei, first it's important to understand a little bit about canine physiology and what Mother Nature intended when she created our furry companions.

While humans are omnivores who can derive energy from eating plants, our canine companions are natural carnivores, which means they derive their energy and nutrient requirements from eating a diet consisting mainly or exclusively of the flesh of animals, birds or fish.

Although dogs can survive on an omnivorous diet this does not mean it is the best diet for them. Unlike humans, who are equipped with wide, flat molars for grinding grains, vegetables and other plant-based materials, canine teeth are all pointed because they are designed to rip, shred and tear into meat and bone.

Another obvious consideration when choosing an appropriate food source for our furry friends is the fact that every canine is born equipped with powerful jaws and neck muscles for the specific purpose of being able to pull down and tear apart their hunted prey.

Photo Credit: Lauren J Alexander of Lauren's Shar-Pei

The structure of the jaw of every canine is such that it opens widely to hold large pieces of meat and bone, while the mechanics of a dog's jaw permits only vertical (up and down) movement that is designed for crushing.

The Canine Digestive Tract

A dog's digestive tract is short and simple and designed to move their natural choice of food (hide, meat and bone) quickly through their systems.

The canine digestive system is simply unable to properly break down vegetable matter, which is why whole vegetables look pretty much the same going into your dog as they do coming out the other end.

Given the choice, most dogs would never choose to eat plants and grains, or vegetables and fruits, over meat; however, we humans continue to feed them a kibble-based diet that contains high amounts of vegetables, fruits and grains with low amounts of meat.

Part of this is because we've been taught that it's a healthy, balanced diet for humans, and therefore we believe that it must be the same for our dogs, and part of this is because all the fillers that make up our dog's foods are less expensive and easier to process than meat.

How much healthier and long lived might our beloved Shar-Pei be if, instead of largely ignoring nature's design for our canine companions, we chose to feed them whole, unprocessed, species-appropriate food with the main ingredient being meat?

Whatever you decide to feed your dog, keep in mind that just as too much wheat, other grains and fillers in our human diet causes a detrimental effect on our health, the same can be very true for our best fur friends.

Our dogs are also suffering from many of the same life-threatening diseases that are rampant in our human society as a direct result of consuming a diet high in genetically altered, impure, processed and packaged foods.

The BARF Diet

Raw feeding advocates believe that the ideal diet for their dog is one that would be very similar to what a dog living in the wild would have access to, and these canine guardians are often opposed to feeding their dog any sort of commercially manufactured pet foods.

On the other hand, those opposed to feeding their dogs a raw or Biologically Appropriate Raw Food (BARF) diet believe that the risks associated with food-borne illnesses during the handling and feeding of raw meats outweigh the purported benefits.

Raw meats purchased at your local grocery store contain a much higher level of acceptable bacteria than raw food produced for dogs, because the meat purchased for human consumption is meant to be cooked, which will kill any bacteria.

This means that canine guardians feeding their dogs a raw food diet can be quite certain that commercially prepared raw foods sold in pet stores will be safer than raw meats purchased in grocery stores.

Many guardians of high-energy, working breed dogs will agree that their dogs thrive on a raw or BARF diet and strongly believe that the potential benefits of feeding a dog a raw food diet are many, including:

- Healthy, shiny coats
- Decreased shedding

- Fewer allergy problems
- Healthier skin
- Cleaner teeth
- Fresher breath
- Higher energy levels
- Improved digestion
- Smaller stools
- Strengthened immune system
- Increased mobility in arthritic pets
- General increase or improvement in overall health

All dogs, whether working breed or lap dogs, are amazing athletes in their own right, and therefore every dog deserves to be fed the best food available.

A raw diet is a direct evolution of what dogs ate before they became our domesticated pets and we turned toward commercially prepared, easy-to-serve dry dog food that required no special storage or preparation.

The Dehydrated Diet

Dehydrated dog food comes in both raw and cooked forms, and these foods are usually air-dried to reduce moisture to the level where bacterial growth is inhibited.

The appearance of dehydrated dog food is very similar to dry kibble, and the typical feeding methods include adding warm water before serving, which makes this type of diet both healthy for our dogs and convenient for us to serve.

Dehydrated recipes are made from minimally processed fresh whole foods to create a healthy and nutritionally balanced meal that will meet or exceed the dietary requirements for healthy canines.

Dehydrating removes only the moisture from the fresh ingredients, which usually means that because the food has not already been cooked at a high temperature, more of the overall nutrition is retained. A dehydrated diet is a convenient way to feed your dog a nutritious diet, because all you have to do is add warm water and wait five minutes while the food re-hydrates so your Shar-Pei can enjoy a warm meal.

Bobbie Libman of Mikobi Shar-Pei adds: "I feed Honest Kitchen over the kibble which is freeze-dried raw. They have a variety of flavors including some grain-free products. You can find them online at www.honestkitchen.com. This product can also be fed as a complete diet. Personally, I prefer to add to the kibble since I think it's important that dogs have something to chew which also helps to keep the teeth strong and clean."

The Kibble Diet

While many canine guardians are starting to take a closer look at the food choices they are making for their furry companions, there is no mistaking that the convenience and relative economy of dry dog food kibble, which had its beginnings in the 1940s, continues to be the most popular pet food choice for most humans.

While feeding a high-quality, bagged kibble diet that has been flavored to appeal to dogs and supplemented with vegetables and fruits to appeal to humans may keep most every Shar-Pei companion happy and healthy, you will need to decide whether this is the best diet for them.

The First Lessons

Do not give a puppy full run of the house until the dog is housebroken. Use a baby gate to keep your pet in a controlled area, both to protect the puppy and your home. There are all kinds of hazards in your environment that, while normal for you to navigate, are dangerous for a little dog, like staircases and landings.

Baby gates, depending on size and configuration, sell in a range of $25-$100 / £14.87-£59.46.

Any time you leave the house, put the puppy in his crate until you return.

Housebreaking

To effectively housebreak your puppy, the crate is an indispensable tool. Dogs instinctively hold their need to eliminate when they are inside their "den." When you leave the house, crate your pet, immediately taking him out upon your return.

Housebreaking also requires you to set and maintain a daily routine. Highly intelligent breeds like the Shar-Pei respond especially well to regularity, and for this reason are much easier to train.

The dog's feeding schedule dictates the frequency of his required trips outside. As he gets older, the number of trips per day will decrease. In the beginning, however, realize that puppies don't yet have full control of their bladder and bowels. Be flexible. When young dogs get too excited, "stuff" happens.

Adult dogs typically go out 3-4 times per day: in the morning, an hour after each meal, and before bedtime. Puppies go out much more often. Never wait more than 15 minutes after a meal to take a young dog outside or you will be sorry.

Photo Credit: Joy & Richard Bayliss of Tianshan Shar Pei

Use positive reinforcement and encouraging phrases to support correct elimination habits. Do not punish a dog for an accident. Your pet does not have the ability to associate the punishment with the incident. Your anger will leave him uncomfortable and anxious. He'll know he did something wrong, but he won't understand what.

When you do catch the puppy going inside the house, say "bad dog," but don't go on and on. Use an enzymatic cleaner to remove the odor and the stain. Once the mess has been cleaned up, go straight back to the normal routine.

Nature's Miracle Stain and Odor Removal is an excellent and affordable enzymatic cleaner at just $5 / £2.97 per 32-ounce / 0.9-liter bottle.

The following are methods that you may or may not have considered, all of which have their own merits, including:

• Bell training

- Exercise pen training
- Free training
- Kennel training

All of these are effective methods, so long as you add in the one critical and often missing "wild card" ingredient, which is "human training."

When you bring home your new Shar-Pei puppy, they will be relying upon your guidance to teach them what they need to learn, and when it comes to housetraining, the first thing the human guardian needs to learn is that the puppy is not being bad when they pee or poop inside.

They are just responding to the call of Mother Nature, and you need to pay close attention right from the very beginning, because it's entirely possible to teach a puppy to go to the bathroom outside in less than a week. Therefore, if your puppy is making bathroom "mistakes," blame yourself, not your puppy.

Check in with yourself and make sure your energy remains consistently calm and patient and that you exercise plenty of compassion and understanding while you help your new puppy learn the bathroom rules. Don't clean up after your puppy with them watching, as this makes the puppy believe you are there to clean up after them, making you lower in the dog pack order.

While your puppy is still growing, on average they can hold it approximately one hour for every month of their age. This means that if your 3-month-old puppy has been happily snoozing for two to three hours, as soon as they wake up, they will need to go outside.

Some of the first indications or signs that your puppy needs to be taken outside to relieve themselves will be when you see them:

- sniffing around
- circling
- looking for the door
- whining, crying or barking
- acting agitated

During the early stages of potty training, adding treats as an extra incentive can be a good way to reinforce how happy you are that your puppy is learning to relieve themselves in the right place. Slowly, treats can be removed and replaced with your happy praise, or you can give your puppy a treat after they are back inside.

Next, now that you have a new puppy in your life, you will want to be flexible with respect to adapting your schedule to meet their internal clocks to quickly teach your Shar-Pei puppy their new bathroom routine.

This means not leaving your puppy alone for endless hours at a time, because firstly, they are pack animals that need companionship and your direction at all times, plus long periods alone will result in the disruption of the potty training schedule you have worked hard to establish.

If you have no choice but to leave your puppy alone for many hours, make sure that you place them in a paper-lined room or pen where they can relieve themselves without destroying your newly installed hardwood or favorite carpet.

Remember, your Shar-Pei is a growing puppy with a bladder and bowels over which they do not yet have complete control.

Bell Training

A very easy way to introduce your new Shar-Pei puppy to house training is to begin by teaching them how to ring a doorbell whenever they need to go outside. A further benefit of training your puppy to ring a bell is that you will not have to listen to your puppy or dog whining, barking or howling to be let out, and your door will not become scratched up from their nails.

Attach the bell to a piece of ribbon or string and hang it from a door handle or tape it to a doorsill near the door where you will be taking your puppy out when they need to relieve themselves. The string will need to be long enough so that your puppy can easily reach the bell with their nose or a paw.

Next, each time you take your puppy out to relieve themselves, say the word "out," and use their paw or their nose to ring the bell. Praise them for this "trick" and immediately take them outside. This type of alert system is an easy way to eliminate accidents in the home.

Kennel Training

When you train your Shar-Pei puppy to accept sleeping in their own kennel at nighttime, this will also help to accelerate their potty training. Because no puppy or dog wants to relieve themselves where they sleep, they will hold their bladder and bowels as long as they possibly can.

Presenting them with familiar scents by taking them to the same spot in the yard or the same street corner will help to remind and encourage them that they are outside to relieve themselves.

Use a voice cue to remind your puppy why they are outside, such as "go pee," and always remember to praise them every time they relieve themselves in the right place, so that they quickly understand what you expect of them.

Exercise Pen Training

The exercise pen is a transition from kennel-only training and will be helpful for those times when you may have to leave your Shar-Pei puppy for more hours than they can reasonably be expected to hold it.

Exercise pens are usually constructed of wire sections that you can put together in whatever shape you desire, and the pen needs to be large enough to hold your puppy's kennel in one half of the pen, while the other half will be lined with newspapers or pee pads.

Place your Shar-Pei puppy's food and water dishes next to the kennel and leave the kennel door open (or take it off) so they can wander in and out whenever they wish to eat or drink or go to the papers or pee pads if they need to relieve themselves.

Because they are already used to sleeping inside their kennel, they will not want to relieve themselves inside the area where they sleep. Therefore, your puppy will naturally go to the other half of the pen to relieve themselves.

Free Training

If you would rather not confine your young Shar-Pei puppy to one or two rooms in your home and will be allowing them to freely range about your home anywhere they wish during the day, this is considered free training.

Never get upset or scold a puppy for having an accident inside the home, because this will result in teaching your puppy to be afraid of you and to only relieve themselves in secret places or when you're not watching.

If you catch your Shar-Pei puppy making a mistake, all that is necessary is for you to calmly say "no" and quickly scoop them up and take them outside or to their indoor bathroom area.

The Shar-Pei is not a difficult puppy to housebreak, and they will generally do very well when you start them off with "puppy pee pads" that you will move closer and closer to the same door that you always use when taking them outside. This way, they will quickly learn to associate going to this door with when they need to relieve themselves.

Territorial Marking

Any dog with an intact reproductive system, regardless of gender, will mark territory by urinating. In most cases this behavior occurs outdoors, but if the dog is upset about something, marking can also occur inside. Again, use an enzymatic cleaner to remove the odor. Otherwise, the dog may be attracted to use the same location again. Territorial marking occurs most frequently with intact males. As a long-term solution, have the dog neutered.

Do not think that territorial marking is caused by poor house training. The two behaviors are completely unrelated and driven by different reactions and urges.

Separation Anxiety

Separation anxiety may be expressed in varying ways: howling, barking, chewing, and urinating or defecating in the house. When the dog realizes you are about to leave the house, you may see behaviors like uncontrollable jumping or nervous cowering. The dog may begin to follow you around and do everything possible to get your attention as his discomfort escalates.

Although some Shar-Pei are laid back and calm, historically the breed is standoffish and aloof with strangers, which can translate to separation anxiety when they are away from their family.

The best thing you can do to get ahead of separation anxiety from the beginning is to crate train your puppy. If a dog feels that he has a safe place, you have given him an essential coping mechanism against anxiety. Far from being a punishment, the crate is a comfort to your pet.

Grooming

Do not allow yourself to get caught in the "my Shar-Pei doesn't like it" trap, which is an excuse many owners will use to avoid regular grooming sessions. When you allow your dog to dictate whether they will permit a grooming session, you are setting a dangerous precedent.

Once you have bonded with your dog, they love to be tickled, rubbed and scratched in certain favorite places. This is why grooming is a great source of pleasure and a way to bond with your pet.

The Shar-Pei is a basically clean dog without any heavy odor. Unless something has happened like a good roll in the mud, your dog should only need a bath every 3 months or so. Bathing a Shar-Pei more frequently may irritate his skin.

The horse coat needs to be bathed more frequently than the brush coat – the shorter hair tends to get greasy faster.

Cate Stewart of Nordic Star Shar-Pei shatters another commonly held myth about the Shar-Pei: "It is a fallacy about drying between wrinkles. Adult dogs aren't that wrinkly and the wrinkling will never be so heavy that this is necessary. They are prone to yeast skin infections but mainly from ears and between toes. The drying and powdering between wrinkles seems to be one of those myths about the breed that won't die!"

Take care not to get the dog's head or ears wet. Clean the head and face with a warm washcloth. Rinse all shampoo from the coat with fresh, clean water. Do not allow any residue to remain on the dog's skin, especially deep in the wrinkles and folds.

The Shar-Pei coat is harsh and short. It should not be trimmed. Weekly brushing with a short rubber brush or a grooming mitt will keep the coat in good shape. Shedding is minimal with the breed except when they blow their coat (usually twice a year), and shedding can be heavy at that time. A shedding tool is recommended then. (Brushes are inexpensive, costing less than $15 / £9.)

Brushing sessions are also a great chance to examine your pet's skin for any unusual growths, lumps, bumps, or wounds. Be sure to check around the eyes, in and behind the ears, and around the mouth.

Your vigilance is the basis for solid, long-term healthcare for your dog. Get in the habit of looking for discharge from the eyes or nose. Watch the ears for accumulated debris or a foul odor that signals the presence of parasites.

If you do work with a professional groomer, find one who has experience with Shar-Pei. Expect, on average, to pay $25-$50 / £15-£30 per session.

How to Bathe Your Shar-Pei

The earlier you start bathing your Shar-Pei, the easier it is going to be – if your Shar-Pei gets used to it as a puppy then he will be less difficult to handle later. Follow the tips below:

1.)   Fill a bathtub with several inches of warm water.
2.)   Place your Shar-Pei in the tub and wet down his coat. Use a bath mat so they don't slip and slide.
3.)   Apply a dollop of dog shampoo to your hands and work it into your Shar-Pei's coat, starting at the base of his neck.
4.)   Work the shampoo into the back, down his legs and tail.
5.)   Rinse your dog well, getting rid of all the soap.
6.)   Towel dry to remove as much moisture as possible.
7.)   If desired, use a hair dryer on the cool setting.

It is very important that you avoid getting water in your Shar-Pei's ears and eyes. If your Shar-Pei's ears get wet, dry them carefully with a cotton ball to prevent infection.

Bobbie Libman of Mikobi Shar-Pei has this tip: "I began using Chamois cloths to dry the dogs. It works great and they don't have to be laundered as much. They just air dry, and can be washed in the washing machine. However, DO NOT put them in the dryer. I have found that they work much better than towels."

Nail Trimming

Most Shar-Pei do not like to have their nails trimmed, as they have sensitive nails, but this is a regular bit of maintenance that cannot be ignored. Their nails should be kept as short as possible. That procedure should start at a very young age since they do not like their feet touched. Start early and do it weekly. They do best without tight restraint.

Depending on your dog's reaction, you can perform this chore yourself with an appropriate clipper. I prefer models with plier grips for ease of handling. Most brands sell for less than $20 / £11.88.

Even better than a nail clipper is the electric Dremel™ tool, since there is a lesser chance of cutting into the quick. In addition, your dog's nails will be smooth, without the sharp edges clipping alone can create.

NOTE: never use a regular Dremel™ tool, as it will be too high speed and will burn your dog's toenails. Only use a slow-speed Dremel™, such as Model 7300-PT Pet Nail Grooming Tool (approx. $40/£20). You can also purchase the flexible hose attachment for the Dremel™, which is much easier to handle and can be held like a pencil.

Position your dog on an elevated surface. You need good visibility and working room. Don't be surprised if you have to ask someone to help you. The goal is to snip off the tip of each nail at a 45-degree angle. Be careful not to cut into the vascular quick at the base. You'll hurt the dog and the nail will bleed heavily.

If your Shar-Pei absolutely refuses to cooperate, which is a real possibility, you may need to have your pet's nails trimmed at the vet's or by a professional groomer.

Anal Glands

Blocked anal glands are common in dogs, evidenced by telltale scooting of the backside on the carpet or ground and a strong, foul odor. The blockage can only be relieved by expressing the glands. Unless this is done, an abscess may form. The delicate nature of this procedure should be left to a groomer or performed in the vet's office.

Photo Credit: Owner Kerry Audley. Note that the dog on the left is an example of a bear coat and the one on the right is displaying a pattern in its coat. A bear coat or pattern is considered a major fault in a show dog but nevertheless they do make excellent companion and performance dogs.

Fleas and Ticks

Fleas and ticks are often detected on a dog during grooming. While no one wants "passengers" on their pet, the occasional flea is just pretty much part of living your life with a dog. It happens. Deal with it. Move on.

Never put a commercial flea product on a puppy of less than 12 weeks of age and only use such products on adult dogs with extreme caution. The major flea control brands contain pyrethrum, which has been linked to long-term neurological damage. The chemical can be deadly for small dogs. Instead, use a standard canine shampoo and warm water. Bathe your dog, and use a fine-toothed flea comb to work through the coat and trap the fleas. Kill the live fleas by submerging the comb in hot soapy water.

Wash all of the dog's bedding and any soft materials with which he has come in contact. Check all areas of the house where the dog sleeps for accumulations of "flea dirt," which is dried blood excreted by adult fleas. To make sure that there are no remaining eggs that will hatch and re-infest the dog, wash these materials and surfaces daily for at least a week.

For ticks, coat the parasite with a thick layer of petroleum jelly and wait 5 minutes. The tick will suffocate and its jaw will release, allowing you to pluck it away from the skin with a straight motion using a pair of tweezers. Don't jerk the tick off! The head will stay in place and, if the tick is still alive, continue to burrow into the skin, creating a painful sore.

Collar or Harness/Standard Leash or Retractable?

Shar-Pei are only moderately active dogs. They can live happily in any residential setting, including apartments and condos. Just make sure that your pet gets a 20-minute walk per day and he'll be perfectly happy.

As a staple of dog ownership, the traditional collar that fits around the neck is almost iconic, but I don't like this arrangement. I wouldn't want to go through life with something around my neck, especially with a leash attached, which with the mildest tug can create a choking sensation.

I prefer the on-body harness restraints that look like vests and offer a point of attachment between the dog's shoulders. The positioning affords excellent control without placing pressure on the neck. Young dogs accept these harnesses very well and are less likely to strain on the lead during walks.

Take your dog with you to get the best fit since sizing is difficult to guess. I've seen dogs as large as 14 lbs. / 6.35 kg take an "Extra Small." The fit really depends on build, more than weight. Most of these harnesses, regardless of size, sell for $20 - $25 / £11.88 - £14.85.

Leash type is really a matter of personal preference. I use both fixed and retractable leads. Some facilities, like groomers, vet clinics, and dog daycares won't allow retractable because they create a trip-and-fall hazard for other human clients. Fixed-length leashes sell for as little as $5 / £2.97, while retractable leads are priced under $15 / £8.91.

Any young dog has to learn to respect the leash. You do not create this respect by jerking or dragging at the lead, even when a stubborn dog like a Shar-Pei refuses to budge or insists on going in the "wrong" direction. When he does that, pick him up, move to a new position, and start the walk over again. You must always convey that you are the one in charge.

Shar-Pei definitely have a mind of their own, and they aren't so invested in their daily walk that they won't run the risk of being denied the pleasure like some breeds. It's always best if your pet associates the lead with a positive adventure out in the world, but you have to stay in the driver's seat.

Reinforce good behavior on walks by praising your pet and offering him treats as a reward for obedience. As part of the routine, teach your Shar-Pei to sit by issuing the command

and simultaneously pointing down. Do not attach the lead to the harness until the dog obeys. Wait several seconds and then start the walk. If your dog jerks or pulls at the leash, stop, pick up your pet, and start over from the sit command.

The Importance of Basic Commands

Any young dog will benefit from attending a basic obedience class. Although stubborn, a Shar-Pei, like any dog, is eager to please his master. That's simply the nature of a pack animal. If you give your dog consistent direction and a clear command language, you will have much greater success with training.

Shar-Pei have the ability to assimilate about 165-200 words. They cannot, however, attach more than one meaning to any of those words. You must use the same command if you expect the same desirable response. If your dog barks, tell him to be "quiet." If he picks something up, say "drop it." For problem jumping, tell him to get "down." Pick a set of words and stick with them, using a tone of clear authority.

Play Time and Tricks

In teaching any dog tricks, play to a natural tendency the dog displays and then work to extend and change the behavior until it becomes a "trick." Shar-Pei are extremely loyal to their humans. They are intelligent, but so stubborn you may have to give in to the dog's version of what you want him to do.

In selecting toys, don't choose any soft item that can be easily shredded, especially those made of rubber. If your pet swallows the pieces, the dog can choke or develop an intestinal blockage. Stay away from toys with "squeakers." Nylabones are a tried and true favorite and they are inexpensive at $1-$5 / £0.59-£2.97 range.

Playtime is important, especially for a dog's natural desire to chase. Try channeling this instinct with toys and games. If a dog has no stimulation and has nothing to chase, they can start to chase their own tail, which can lead to problems.

Toys can be used to simulate the dog's natural desire to hunt. For example, when they catch a toy, they will often shake it and bury their teeth into it, simulating the killing of their prey.

Allow your dog to fulfill a natural desire to chew. This comes from historically catching their prey and then chewing the carcass. Providing chews or bones can prevent your dog from destroying your home.

Playing with your dog is not only a great way of getting them to use up their energy, but it is also a great way of bonding with them as they have fun. Dogs love to chase and catch balls, just make sure that the ball is too large to be swallowed.

Deer antlers are wonderful toys for Shar-Pei. Most love them. They do not smell, are all-natural and do not stain or splinter. I recommend the antlers that are not split, as they last longer.

Photo Credit: Kathy Torres & Marie Bradley of Maka Shar Pei

Chapter 6 - Training and Problem Behaviors

Shar-Pei have a reputation for being highly affectionate dogs. They are not prone to barking, do well in almost any living arrangement, and have low needs for exercise and society beyond the company of their people. They are good watchdogs, but not terribly aggressive, and though stubborn, can be very well trained.

Bear in mind, however, that any dog can develop poor behaviors, which may or may not be directed at people. Sometimes your dog may be reacting to a perceived threat you don't even understand has occurred by snapping, lunging, pushing, barking, or baring of the teeth.

Photo Credit: Marilyn Vinson of China Fleet Shar-Pei

All of these problems can be blunted or eliminated by proper socialization of young dogs. Shar-Pei tend to be aloof with strangers, but they are also adaptable. The more situations to which you expose your pet, the better adjusted he will be.

Enroll your pet in a training class and expose him to new sights, sounds, people, and places. Be attentive to the behavior of your own dog as well as what's going on around you. Often in a public setting the best way to ensure there are no problems is to avoid other dogs altogether — not because your pet can't behave, but because another dog owner isn't in control of his animal.

Dog Whispering

Many people can be confused when they need professional help with their dog, because for many years, if you needed help with your dog, you contacted a "dog trainer" or took your dog to "puppy classes" where your dog would learn how to sit or stay.

The difference between a dog trainer and a dog whisperer would be that a "dog trainer" teaches a dog how to perform certain tasks, and a "dog whisperer" alleviates behavior problems by teaching humans what they need to do to keep their particular dog happy.

Often, depending on how soon the guardian has sought help, this can mean that the dog in question has developed some pretty serious issues, such as aggressive barking, lunging, biting or attacking other dogs, pets or people.

Dog whispering is often an emotional roller coaster ride for the humans involved, and unveils many truths when they finally realize that it has been their actions (or inactions) that have likely caused the unbalanced behavior that their dog is now displaying.

Once solutions are provided, the relief for both dog and human can be quite cathartic when they realize that with the correct direction, they can indeed live a happy life with their dog.

All specific methods of training, such as "clicker training," fall outside of what every dog needs to be happy, because training your dog to respond to a clicker, which you can easily do on your own, and then letting them sleep in your bed, eat from your plate and any other multitude of things humans allow, are what makes the dog unbalanced and causes behavior problems.

I always say to people, don't wait until you have a severe problem before getting some dog whispering or professional help of some sort, because, "With the proper training, Man can learn to be dog's best friend."

Rewarding Unwanted Behavior

It is very important to recognize that any attention paid to an out-of-control, adolescent puppy, even negative attention, is likely to be exciting and rewarding for your Shar-Pei puppy.

Chasing after a puppy when they have taken something they shouldn't have, picking them up when barking or showing aggression, pushing them off when they jump on other people, or yelling when they refuse to come when called are all forms of attention that can actually be rewarding for most puppies.

It will be your responsibility to provide structure for your puppy, which will include finding acceptable and safe ways to allow your puppy to vent their energy without being destructive or harmful to others.

The worst thing you can do when training your Shar-Pei is to yell at him or use punishment. Positive reinforcement training methods – that is, rewarding your dog for good behavior – are infinitely more effective than negative reinforcement – training by punishment.

It is important when training your Shar-Pei that you do not allow yourself to get frustrated. If you feel yourself starting to get angry, take a break and come back to the training session later.

Why is punishment-based training so bad? Think about it this way – your dog should listen to you because he wants to please you, right?

If you train your dog using punishment, he could become fearful of you and that could put a damper on your relationship with him. Do your dog and yourself a favor by using positive reinforcement.

Teaching Basic Commands

When it comes to training your Shar-Pei, you have to start off slowly with the basic commands. The most popular basic commands for dogs include sit, down, stay and come.

Sit

This is the most basic and one of the most important commands you can teach your Shar-Pei.

1.)   Stand in front of your Shar-Pei with a few small treats in your pocket.

2.)   Hold one treat in your dominant hand and wave it in front of your Shar-Pei's nose so he gets the scent.

3.)   Give the "Sit" command.

4.)   Move the treat upward and backward over your Shar-Pei's head so he is forced to raise his head to follow it.

5.)   In the process, his bottom will lower to the ground.

6.)   As soon as your Shar-Pei's bottom hits the ground, praise him and give him the treat.

7.)   Repeat this process several times until your dog gets the hang of it and responds consistently.

Photo Credit: Barbara LaVere of Tzo Wen Shar-Pei and Tammy Bohlke Xin Jin Shar-Pei

Down

After the "Sit" command, "Down" is the next logical command to teach because it is a progression from "Sit."

1.)   Kneel in front of your Shar-Pei with a few small treats in your pocket.

2.)   Hold one treat in your dominant hand and give your Shar-Pei the "Sit" command.

3.)   Reward your Shar-Pei for sitting, then give him the "Down" command.

4.)   Quickly move the treat down to the floor between your Shar-Pei's paws.

5.)   Your dog will follow the treat and should lie down to retrieve it.

6.)   Praise and reward your Shar-Pei when he lies down.

7.)   Repeat this process several times until your dog gets the hang of it and responds consistently.

Come

It is very important that your Shar-Pei responds to a "come" command, because there may come a time when you need to get his attention and call him to your side during a dangerous situation (such as him running around too close to traffic).

1.)   Put your Shar-Pei on a short leash and stand in front of him.

2.)   Give your Shar-Pei the "come" command, then quickly take a few steps backward away from him.

3.)   Clap your hands and act excited, but do not repeat the "come" command.

4.)   Keep moving backwards in small steps until your Shar-Pei follows and comes to you.

5.)   Praise and reward your Shar-Pei and repeat the process.

6.)   Over time you can use a longer leash or take your Shar-Pei off the leash entirely.

7.)   You can also start by standing farther away from your Shar-Pei when you give the "come" command.

8.)   If your Shar-Pei doesn't come to you immediately, you can use the leash to pull him toward you.

Stay

This command is very important because it teaches your Shar-Pei discipline – not only does it teach your Shar-Pei to stay, but it also forces him to listen and pay attention to you.

1.)   Find a friend to help you with this training session.

2.)   Have your friend hold your Shar-Pei on the leash while you stand in front of the dog.

3.)   Give your Shar-Pei the "sit" command and reward him for responding correctly.

4.)   Give your dog the "stay" command while holding your hand out like a "stop" sign.

5.)   Take a few steps backward away from your dog and pause for 1 to 2 seconds.

6.)   Step back toward your Shar-Pei, then praise and reward your dog.

7.)   Repeat the process several times, then start moving back a little farther before you return to your dog.

Beyond Basic Training

Once your Shar-Pei has a firm grasp on the basics, you can move on to teaching him additional commands. You can also add distractions to the equation to reinforce your dog's mastery of the commands. The end goal is to ensure that your Shar-Pei responds to your command each and every time – regardless of distractions and anything else he might rather be doing. This is incredibly important, because there may come a time when your dog is in a dangerous situation and if he doesn't respond to your command, he could get hurt.

After your Shar-Pei has started to respond correctly to the basic commands on a regular basis, you can start to incorporate distractions.

If you previously conducted your training sessions indoors, you might consider moving them outside where your dog could be distracted by various sights, smells and sounds.

One thing you might try is to give your dog the Stay command and then toss a toy nearby that will tempt him to break his Stay. Start by tossing the toy a good distance from him and wait a few seconds before you release him to play.

Eventually you will be able to toss a toy right next to your dog without him breaking his Stay until you give him permission to do so.

Incorporating Hand Signals

Teaching your Shar-Pei to respond to hand signals in addition to verbal commands is very useful – you never know when you will be in a situation where your dog might not be able to hear you.

To start out, choose your dominant hand to give the hand signals, and hold a small treat in that hand while you are training your dog – this will encourage your dog to focus on your hand during training, and it will help to cement the connection between the command and the hand signal.

To begin, give your dog the Sit or Down command while holding the treat in your dominant hand and give the appropriate hand signal – for Sit you might try a closed fist, and for Down you might place your hand flat, parallel to the ground.

When your dog responds correctly, give him the treat. You will need to repeat this process many times in order for your dog to form a connection between both the verbal command and the hand signal with the desired behavior.

Eventually, you can start to remove the verbal command from the equation – use the hand gesture every time, but start to use the verbal command only half the time.

Once your dog gets the hang of this, you should start to remove the food reward from the equation. Continue to give your dog the hand signal for each command, and occasionally use the verbal command just to remind him.

You should start to phase out the food rewards, however, by offering them only half the time. Progressively lessen the use of the food reward, but continue to praise your dog for performing the behavior correctly so he learns to repeat it.

Teaching Distance Commands

In addition to getting your dog to respond to hand signals, it is also useful to teach him to respond to your commands even when you are not directly next to him.

This may come in handy if your dog is running around outside and gets too close to the street – you should be able to give him a Sit or Down command so he stops before he gets into a dangerous situation.

Teaching your dog distance commands is not difficult, but it does require some time and patience.

To start, give your Shar-Pei a brief refresher course of the basic commands while you are standing or kneeling right next to him.

Next, give your dog the Sit and Stay commands, then move a few feet away before you give the Come command.

Repeat this process, increasing the distance between you and your dog before giving him the Come command. Be sure to praise and reward your dog for responding appropriately when he does so.

Once your dog gets the hang of coming on command from a distance, you can start to incorporate other commands.

One method of doing so is to teach your dog to sit when you grab his collar. To do so, let your dog wander freely and every once in a while walk up and grab his collar while giving the Sit command.

After a few repetitions, your dog should begin to respond with a Sit when you grab his collar, even if you do not give the command.

Gradually, you can increase the distance from which you come to grab his collar and give him the command.

After your dog starts to respond consistently when you come from a distance to grab his collar, you can start giving the Sit command without moving toward him.

It may take your dog a few times to get the hang of it, so be patient. If your dog doesn't Sit right away, calmly walk up to him and repeat the Sit command, but do not grab his collar this time.

Eventually, your dog will get the hang of it, and you can start to practice using other commands like Down and Stay from a distance.

Clicker Training

When it comes to training your Shar-Pei, you are going to be most successful if you maintain consistency. Shar-Pei have a tendency to be a little stubborn, so unless you are very clear with your dog about what your expectations are, he may simply decide not to follow your commands.

A simple way to achieve consistency in training your Shar-Pei is to use the principles of clicker training. Clicker training involves using a small handheld device that makes a clicking noise when you press it between your fingers.

Clicker training is based on the theory of operant conditioning, which helps your dog to make the connection between the desired behavior and the offering of a reward.

Shar-Pei have a natural desire to please, so if they learn that a certain behavior earns your approval, they will be eager to repeat it – clicker training is a great way to help your dog quickly identify the particular behavior you want him to repeat.

All you have to do is give your Shar-Pei a command and, as soon as he performs the behavior, you use the clicker. After you use the clicker, give your dog the reward as you would with any form of positive reinforcement training.

Some of the benefits of clicker training include:

- Very easy to implement – all you need is the clicker.
- Helps your dog form a connection between the command and the desired behavior more quickly.
- You only need to use the clicker until your dog makes the connection, then you can stop.

- May help to keep your dog's attention more effectively if he hears the noise.

Clicker training is just one method of positive reinforcement training that you can consider for training your Shar-Pei.

No matter what method you choose, it is important that you maintain consistency and always praise and reward your dog for responding to your commands correctly so he learns to repeat the behavior.

First Tricks

When teaching your Shar-Pei their first tricks, in order to give them extra incentive, find a small treat that they would do anything to get, and give the treat as a reward to help solidify a good performance.

Most dogs will be extra attentive during training sessions when they know that they will be rewarded with their favorite treats.

If your Shar-Pei is less than six months old when you begin teaching them tricks, keep your training sessions short (no more than 5 or 10 minutes) and make the sessions lots of fun.

As your Shar-Pei becomes an adult, you can extend your sessions, because they will be able to maintain their focus for longer periods of time.

Shake a Paw

Who doesn't love a dog that knows how to shake a paw? This is one of the easiest tricks to teach your Shar-Pei.

Practice every day until they are 100% reliable with this trick, and then it will be time to add another trick to their repertoire.

Most dogs are naturally either right or left pawed. If you know which paw your dog favors, ask them to shake this paw.

Find a quiet place to practice, without noisy distractions or other pets, and stand or sit in front of your dog. Place them in the sitting position and hold a treat in your left hand.

Say the command "Shake" while putting your right hand behind their left or right paw and pulling the paw gently toward yourself until you are holding their paw in your hand. Immediately praise them and give them the treat.

Most dogs will learn the "Shake" trick very quickly, and in no time at all, once you put out your hand, your Shar-Pei will immediately lift their paw and put it into your hand, without your assistance or any verbal cue.

Roll Over

You will find that just like your Shar-Pei is naturally either right or left pawed, they will also naturally want to roll either to the right or the left side.

Take advantage of this by asking your dog to roll to the side they naturally prefer. Sit with your dog on the floor and put them in a lie down position.

Hold a treat in your hand and place it close to their nose without allowing them to grab it, and while they are in the lying position, move the treat to the right or left side of their head so that they have to roll over to get to it.

You will quickly see which side they want to naturally roll to; once you see this, move the treat to that side. Once they roll over to that side, immediately give them the treat and praise them.

You can say the verbal cue "Over" while you demonstrate the hand signal motion (moving your right hand in a half circular motion) from one side of their head to the other.

Sit Pretty

While this trick is a little more complicated, and most dogs pick up on it very quickly, remember that this trick requires balance, and every dog is different, so always exercise patience.

Find a quiet space with few distractions and sit or stand in front of your dog and ask them to "Sit."

Have a treat nearby (on a countertop or table) and when they sit, use both of your hands to lift up their front paws into the sitting pretty position, while saying the command "Sit Pretty." Help them balance in this position while you praise them and give them the treat.

Once your Shar-Pei can do the balancing part of the trick quite easily without your help, sit or stand in front of your dog while asking them to "Sit Pretty" and hold the treat above their head, at the level their nose would be when they sit pretty.

If they attempt to stand on their back legs to get the treat, you may be holding the treat too high, which will encourage them to stand up on their back legs to reach it. Go back to the first step and put them back into the "Sit" position and again lift their paws while their backside remains on the floor.

The hand signal for "Sit Pretty" is a straight arm held over your dog's head with a closed fist. Place your Shar-Pei beside a wall when first teaching this trick so that they can use the wall to help their balance.

A young Shar-Pei puppy should be able to easily learn these basic tricks before they are six months old, and when you are patient and make your training sessions short and fun for your dog, they will be eager to learn more.

Excessive Jumping

Excessive jumping will quickly earn your dog a bad reputation. Typically this is not a problem with the Shar-Pei, but since they are burly dogs, they can easily knock over small people and children. In fact, if a Shar-Pei does feel the need to encounter an intruder, they are much more likely to pin the offender to the ground than to attack viciously.

When excessive jumping occurs, it may well be a dominance display or an example of amplifying separation anxiety. The dog may either see himself as higher in the pack hierarchy than you, or he may be trying to stop you from leaving the house.

Under all circumstances, be stern in enforcing the no jumping rule. If you are not, you will only confuse your pet. All dogs understand space as a concept. Don't retreat when a dog jumps – step into him and slightly to the side, taking back the area he's trying to claim. You aren't trying to knock your pet down, but this may well happen if he forces the issue.

Your role is to move with slow deliberation and to stay casual, calm, and confident. Control the "bubble" of space around your body and don't let the dog invade that territory. The dog won't anticipate or like your response. It may take a few such encounters, but sending a dominant message will stop a jumper.

Barking Behavior

It is extremely rare for a Shar-Pei to exhibit problem barking. If it does occur, barking can be hugely problematic, leading to conflict with the neighbors and even eviction in apartment settings.

If you have a barker, you have to try to understand why your dog is making so much racket. Loneliness? Boredom? Excitement? Anxiety? Is he seeing / hearing / smelling something? Has something changed that he perceives to be a threat?

Be firm and consistent with your admonitions. Some pet owners use a plant mister or squirt gun as negative reinforcement. Aim for the face, but don't let the stream of water hit the eyes. The only goal is to get your pet's attention and to create a negative association with the bad behavior.

Humane bark collars are also an option. These units release a harmless spray of citronella into the dog's nose triggered by vibrations from the animal's throat. Although somewhat expensive at $100/£60, the system works in almost all cases.

Chewing

Although a natural behavior, chewing to excess is a sign of boredom and anxiety. The answer may be as simple as spending more time with your pet or getting him out of the house for longer periods of time. It's also important to direct the dog's chewing toward proper toys like Nylabones. Confiscate inappropriate items and reprimand the dog, offering him an acceptable chew toy instead.

Digging

Digging is also an expression of fear, anxiety, and/or boredom. While trying to dig his way out and go find you, a determined and anxious digger will destroy furniture and claw through doors.

Again, increase the dog's exercise time. If giving your dog more attention doesn't work, consider taking your Shar-Pei to a dog daycare facility so he won't be alone during the day.

Begging

Don't let begging get started in the first place and you won't be faced with trying to stop the behavior! Make "people" food off limits from day one and don't cheat! If you have to take your dog to another part of the house while you are eating, do it. This isn't so much to control your pet as to control yourself. If you can't ignore a pleading set of Shar-Pei eyes, you're the problem, not the dog!

Chasing

Shar-Pei have some residual hunting instincts. They will chase and catch a creature they perceive to be fleeing from them, including cats. Be exceedingly careful about this instinct of the breed.

Keep your pet leashed at all times. Never allow your Shar-Pei off the lead unless you are securely inside a fenced area. Most dogs become so concentrated on the chase, they refuse to come when called.

Biting

On a whole, Shar-Pei are not known to be biters. All puppies nip at each other during play. If your fingers get in the way, you can get nipped as well. Gently curb this kind of rambunctious behavior. What is cute in a little puppy can be a disaster waiting to happen with an adult dog.

A dog bites as a means of primary defense and in reaction to fear or pain. Again, correct socialization will lessen the chances of a Shar-Pei resorting to this behavior. If an adult dog does start to bite, get to the bottom of the issue quickly.

Start with a trip to the vet. The animal may be in pain from an undiagnosed health problem. If that is not the case, enlist the services of a professional trainer immediately.

Chapter 7 – Shar-Pei Health

When your Shar-Pei needs to see his "primary care" physician, you'll take your pet to a vet. On a daily basis, however, you are your dog's real healthcare provider. As the years go by, you will know your Shar-Pei better than anyone.

You will know what is normal. If you think something is wrong, even in the absence of obvious injury or illness, never hesitate to have your dog evaluated. The greater your understanding of preventive health care, the better you will be able to observe your pet and spot potential problems before they become serious.

Your Veterinarian is Your Partner

If you do not have an established relationship with a qualified veterinarian, get recommendations from your breeder or local dog club. Always see the vet for the first time without your Shar-Pei.

Make it clear when you set up the appointment that you are there to meet the doctor and to evaluate the clinic — and that you will pay for the visit. Veterinarians are busy people. Don't waste their time. Prepare your questions in advance and make sure to cover the following points:

- How long has this practice been in operation?
- How many vets are on staff?
- Are any of those doctors specialists? If so, in what area?
- Where do you refer patients if necessary?
- What are your regular hours? emergency hours?
- Are you affiliated with an emergency clinic?
- What specific services does the clinic offer?
- Do you have or can you recommend a groomer?
- May I have an estimated schedule of fees?
- Do you currently treat any Shar-Pei?

Pay attention to what you see and hear. You want to get a sense of the doctor, the facility, and the staff. Look for:

- how the staff interacts with clients
- the visible level of organization
- evidence of engagement with the clientele (office bulletin board, cards and photos displayed, etc.)
- the quality of all visible equipment
- the condition of the waiting area and back rooms
- prominent display of doctors' credentials

Always go with your own "gut." You will know if the place "feels" right. Trust your intuition. If you don't like the "feel" of a clinic, even if it's modern and well-appointed, keep looking. If they make a comment that all Shar-Pei are unhealthy or require eye and ear surgery, all have skin problems, etc., LEAVE and find a vet without those pre-conceived notions.

Your Dog's First Visit to the Vet

When you choose a vet with whom you are comfortable, make a second appointment that will include your Shar-Pei. Take the puppy's medical records with you. Routine procedures during the visit will include:

- temperature
- checking the heart and lungs with a stethoscope
- weighing the dog
- taking basic measurements to chart growth and physical progress

Be prepared to discuss completing your pet's vaccinations and scheduling the surgery to spay or neuter the dog. Write down any questions that occur to you before you get to the clinic!

Vaccinations

Recommended vaccinations begin at 6-7 weeks of age. The standard shots include:

- distemper
- hepatitis
- parvovirus
- parainfluenza
- coronavirus

Boosters are set for 9, 12, and 16 weeks. In some areas a vaccine for Lyme disease starts at 16 weeks with a booster at 18 weeks. The rabies vaccination is administered at 12-16 weeks and then generally every 3 years.

Evaluating for Worms

It is extremely rare for a puppy acquired from a reputable breeder to have parasites. "Worms" are much more common in rescue dogs and strays. If present, roundworms appear as small white granules around the anus. Other types of worms can only be detected through a microscope.

Some parasites, like tapeworms, may be life threatening. Screening tests are important and do not reflect on your perceived care of the dog. If the puppy tests positive, the standard treatment is a deworming agent with a follow-up dose in 10 days.

It's best to take a stool sample at around 6-7 weeks to determine if the dog has worms or giardia. When the results are negative, it is not necessary to deworm them. Some breeders just give them deworming medicine routinely. It's very important a fecal sample be obtained and sent to a recognized lab for testing.

Spaying and Neutering

Standard adoption agreements for pedigreed dogs include a requirement for the puppy to be spayed or neutered, typically before six months of age. This protects the breeder's bloodlines, helps to stem the tide of unwanted pets, and carries significant health benefits.

The surgery reduces aggression and territoriality in males and reduces the risk of prostatic disease or perianal tumors. Neutered males are also less likely to mark territory, or to behave inappropriately against the legs of your visitors.

Spaying eliminates hormonally related mood swings in females and protects them against uterine or ovarian cancer while lowering the risk for breast cancer. It is a complete myth that dogs that have been neutered are more likely to put on weight.

Photo Credit: Andrea Robins of Gumby's Chinese Shar-Pei

"Normal" Health Issues

There are a number of health issues associated with Shar-Pei, which we will discuss shortly under genetic abnormalities. All dogs can face "normal" health-related issues that may require the services of a vet, however, so we'll cover those first.

Any time your pet seems inattentive or lethargic or stops eating and drinking, a trip to the vet is in order. None of these behaviors are normal for a healthy dog.

Diarrhea

All puppies are easily subject to upset stomachs for the simple reason that they get into things they shouldn't, like the kitchen garbage. Any case of diarrhea caused by such indiscriminate snooping should resolve within 24 hours.

Give the dog smaller than normal portions of dry food, no treats, and plenty of fresh, clean water. Do not let the puppy become dehydrated. If the stools are still watery and loose after 24 hours, call the vet.

Use the same strategy of watchful waiting for adult dogs. When episodic diarrhea becomes chronic, it's time to re-evaluate your pet's diet in consultation with your veterinarian.

Dogs with chronic diarrhea are likely getting too much rich, fatty food. The diet will have to be adjusted to include less fat and protein. Some dogs also do better eating small amounts several times a day rather than having 2-3 larger meals.

Allergies may also be the hidden culprit behind chronic diarrhea. Allergies to chicken and turkey are particularly common. A change in diet resolves gastrointestinal upset due to allergies immediately. Many dogs do much better eating foods based on rabbit or duck.

Finally, dogs can suffer diarrhea from bacteria or viruses. If this is the case, your pet will also run a fever and vomit. In these cases, veterinary treatment is absolutely indicated.

Vomiting

Vomiting from an abrupt dietary change or from eating something inappropriate should also resolve within 24 hours. If the dog has unproductive vomiting, regurgitates blood, or can't keep water down, take your pet to the vet immediately.

Dehydration from vomiting occurs faster than in a case of diarrhea, and can be fatal. It is not unusual for a dog under these circumstances to require IV fluids.

Look around the area for anything the dog may have chewed and swallowed that triggered the vomiting. Identifying the culprit can be crucial in pinpointing the best treatment. Other possible causes include: hookworm, roundworm, pancreatitis, diabetes, thyroid disease, kidney disease, liver disease, or a physical blockage.

Bloat

Any dog can suffer from bloat, but some breeds are at higher risk, including the Great Dane, Weimaraner, Saint Bernard, Irish Setter, and the Standard Poodle. All have deep chests and small waists. In mid-sized dogs, the Shar-Pei and the Basset Hound see the highest incidence of bloat.

The condition, which is also known as gastric dilation / volvulus or GDV, can be fatal if the stomach twists and cuts off circulation to the digestive system. The dog then goes into cardiac arrest. Surgical intervention is often attempted, but there is no guarantee of success.

Signs of bloat are often mistaken for digestive gas. They include:

- excessive salivation
- attempted vomiting
- pacing
- whining

Gas reduction products may help early in the attack, but as the stomach swells, it places pressure on the surrounding vital organs and can become large enough to burst. All cases of bloat are a *serious* medical emergency.

Managing Risk Factors

Dogs fed a single large meal of dry food per day are in a higher-risk category. To guard against bloat, feed your pet three times per day and do not allow the animal to drink excessively after eating. Take up your pet's water at mealtime and do not offer it to the dog for at least 30 minutes.

You do not want the dog to be so hungry it gulps while eating, thus ingesting large amounts of air. If the animal then drinks a lot of water, the dry food in the stomach expands, causing discomfort and swelling. It's also important to limit your pet's exercise after meals for at least an hour. A vigorous romp can be dangerous, while a slow walk will promote proper digestion.

In nervous or anxious dogs, stress also contributes to bloat. Stress might be caused by any change in the animal's routine, confrontations with other dogs, or a move to a new home.

Bloat occurs most often in dogs aged 4-7, with attacks timed between 2 a.m. and 6 a.m., roughly 10 hours after the animal's last meal of the day.

Test the dry food you are using by putting a serving in a bowl with water. Let the material expand overnight. If the bulk seems excessive, investigate changing to a premium or organic food.

Also keep an anti-gas medicine with simethicone on hand. (Consult with your veterinarian on correct dosage.) Adding a probiotic to your dog's food can further reduce stomach gas and improve digestive health.

A dog that has survived one attack of bloat is at greater risk for a future episode. Be prepared in the event of an emergency by having copies of your pet's medical records and knowing the location of the nearest emergency vet clinic.

General Signs of Illness

Dogs exhibiting any of the following symptoms should be evaluated by a vet. Never worry about being seen as an alarmist. Most problems can be resolved quickly if the dog is taken in for treatment at the first sign of illness.

Coughing and/or Wheezing

The occasional cough is no reason for concern, but if it lasts more than a week, your pet should be seen by the vet. A cough can be a symptom of:

- kennel cough
- heartworm
- cardiac disease
- bacterial infections
- parasites
- tumors
- or allergies

Kennel cough is an upper respiratory condition that is a form of canine bronchitis. It spreads quickly in poorly ventilated, overcrowded, and warm conditions. The illness presents with a dry, hacking cough. Although kennel cough typically resolves on its own, your vet may suggest a cough suppressant and a humidifier to ease the irritation in your pet's airways.

For coughs of unknown origin, a full medical history will be taken and tests ordered. These will include X-rays and blood work. If necessary, fluid may be drawn from the lungs for additional analysis. It's always important to rule out heartworms as the causal agent.

Photo Credit: Bonnie Stoney of Stoneys Chinese Shar-Pei

A Note on Heartworms

Heartworms (*Dirofilaria Immitis*) are long, thin parasites spread through mosquito bites. The worms infest cardiac tissue, blocking the vessels that supply the heart and causing bleeding. If left untreated, they may cause heart failure.

Symptoms of a heartworm infestation include an intolerance to exercise, coughing, and fainting. Discuss heartworm prevention with your vet, who can advise you about the most effective preventative measures, including vaccines.

Other Warning Signs of Illness

Other warning signs of potential illness of which you should be aware include:

- Unexplained, excessive drooling.
- Excessive consumption of water.
- Increased urination.
- Changes in appetite.
- Weight gain or loss.
- Marked change in levels of activity.
- Disinterest in favorite activities.
- Stiffness and difficulty standing or climbing stairs.
- Sleeping more than normal.
- Excessive shaking of the head (Shar-Pei are head shakers even when healthy).
- Any sores, lumps, or growths.
- Dry, red, or cloudy eyes.

Often the signs of serious illness are subtle. Trust your instincts. If you think something is wrong, do not hesitate to consult with your vet.

Diabetes

Three forms of diabetes are present in dogs: diabetes insipidus, diabetes mellitus, and gestational diabetes. Each is caused by malfunctioning endocrine glands and may be linked to poor diet. Larger dogs are in a higher-risk category.

- *diabetes insipidus* – Low levels of the hormone vasopressin create problems with the regulation of blood glucose, salt, and water.

- *diabetes mellitus* – The most common and dangerous form, seen as in Types I and II. Diabetes mellitus first develops in young dogs and may be referred to as "juvenile," while adult dogs most often suffer from Type II. All cases are treated with insulin.

- *gestational diabetes* – This form occurs in pregnant females and requires the same treatment as diabetes mellitus. Obese dogs are at greater risk.

Blood sugar levels are affected by abnormal insulin production. Under the right conditions, including being overweight, any mammalian species can develop diabetes.

Symptoms of Canine Diabetes

The following behaviors are signs that a dog may have canine diabetes:

- excessive water consumption
- frequent urination
- lethargy / uncharacteristic laziness
- weight gain or loss for no reason

In many cases, however, there are no evident symptoms. Diabetes comes on slowly. Its effects are not always immediately noticeable. Regular check-ups help to detect this disease before it becomes so serious as to be life threatening.

Managing canine diabetes typically includes the use of a special diet. Insulin injections may also be necessary. This may sound daunting, but anyone can learn to give the shots.

Dogs with diabetes live full and normal lives, they just need to see the vet more often to monitor potential heart, eye and circulatory problems. In most cases the dog will develop diabetic cataracts and it can happen quickly. They can go blind quickly. There is a surgery to remove diseased lens of the eyes and replace it with artificial lenses that can restore sight.

Dental Care

Dogs maintain their teeth with chewing. If they don't get enough of this kind of activity, dental problems can develop even early in life, including accumulated plaque and gum disease.

Often the first indication that something is wrong is severe bad breath. Usually gingivitis develops first. Left untreated, it can progress to actual periodontitis. Warning signs of gum disease include:

- unwilling to finish meals
- extreme bad breath
- swelling of the gums
- bleeding gums
- irregularities in the gum line
- plaque build-up
- drooling
- loose teeth

Periodontitis is a bacterial infection. It causes inflammation, gum recession, and possible tooth loss. In order to prevent the infection from spreading to other parts of the body, your vet will first prescribe a thorough cleaning, followed by a course of antibiotics. Symptoms include:

- pus at the gum line
- loss of appetite
- depression
- irritability
- pawing at the mouth
- trouble chewing
- loose or missing teeth
- gastrointestinal upset

During the course of the dental cleaning, other work may be required, including root canals, descaling, and even extractions.

A dog can also suffer from an overgrowth of the gums called Proliferating Gum Disease, which is also a source of inflammation and infection. Other symptoms include:

- thickening and lengthening of the gums
- bleeding
- bad breath
- drooling
- loss of appetite

Again, cleaning, surgery, and antibiotics may all be required.

Home Dental Care

To get ahead of potential dental problems, there are numerous products you can use at home with your Shar-Pei. Additives in the dog's water can help to break up tartar and plaque, but not all dogs can tolerate these mixtures without stomach upset. Dental sprays and wipes are an option, but gentle gum massage may be all that's needed to break up plaque and tartar.

Most owners use some kind of dental chew because it serves the dual purpose of being both preventive dental care and a dog treat.

Greenies Dental Chews for Dogs are popular and easy on the digestion. Dogs love them! The treats come in different sizes and are priced in a range of $7 / £4.21 for 22 "Teeny Greenies" and $25 / £15 for 17 Large Greenies.

Photo Credit: Barbara LaVere of Tzo Wen Shar-Pei

The best protection for your dog's oral health is the same one you use — brushing, but with a canine-specific toothbrush and toothpaste. NEVER use human toothpaste. Fluoride is toxic to dogs.

Some canine toothbrushes are just smaller versions of the ones we use, but I prefer the brushes that just fit over the end of your finger. They offer terrific control and are easier to handle.

Like most things with a Shar-Pei, the dog will either be completely cooperative or refuse to get onboard at all. There seems to be little middle ground with the breed on such issues. If you can get the dog comfortable with having your hands in its mouth, the fingertip brushes are an unobtrusive addition to massaging the gums with just your fingers. Many vets say if you can simply manage to smear toothpaste on the animal's teeth, you're improving your pet's dental health.

Always try to brush the dog's teeth when he's a little tired and more likely to be cooperative. Don't do anything that will stress your pet. Use small circular motions. Stop if your pet seems to be getting antsy or annoyed. Better to spread a complete brushing out over two or three sessions than to create a negative association in your dog's mind.

No matter how much dental care you can perform at home, always have the dog's mouth examined annually in the vet's office. Exams not only help to keep the teeth and gums healthy, they create an opportunity to check for the presence of other problems, including cancerous growths.

The Matter of Genetic Abnormalities

Potential health conditions associated with Shar-Pei include:

- hip and elbow dysplasia
- patellar luxation
- hypothyroidism
- entropion

- retinal dysplasia
- glaucoma
- allergies
- skin fold infection (rare)
- chronic ear infections by yeast
- Shar-Pei fever
- renal amyloidosis and kidney failure
- more prone to cancers than many other breeds

There is no reliable way to predict if a puppy is free of any of these issues, which makes it all the more imperative that you obtain your pet from a reputable breeder.

In the United States, for instance, The Chinese Shar-Pei Club of America participates in the Canine Health Information Center (CHIC), which awards certification that dogs are free of hip, elbow, patellar, and thyroid problems. The Canine Eye Registry Foundation supplies similar verification that a dog is free of eye problems.

Breeders that are serious about cultivating the healthiest animals possible are able to produce this kind of independent certification, and the results (in the case of the CHIC) are published in a database.

Hip and Elbow Dysplasia

Many breeds, including the Shar-Pei, suffer from hip and elbow dysplasia either as a consequence of a genetic malformation of the ball and socket joints or due to an injury.

The dysplasia takes on one of two forms. The fit of the joint is too tight, restricting motion, or it is chronically loose, causing repetitive dislocations. Either can vary in intensity from a mild annoyance to a painful and debilitating condition.

The first symptom of dysplasia is a hopping, abnormal gait or limp than can appear any time from four months through old age, although signs are not always apparent.

Elbow dysplasia is twice as common in the Shar-Pei as hip dysplasia.

Conservative treatment with pain medication and anti-inflammatory drugs may be possible, but in severe cases, surgery is often indicated, especially if a secondary case of arthritis manifests.

Canine Arthritis

Canine arthritis, like that in humans, is a debilitating degeneration of the joints. The cartilage breaks down, leading to bone-on-bone friction. This creates considerable pain and a restricted range of motion.

Treatments for dogs are the same as those used with humans. Aspirin addresses pain and inflammation, while supplements like glucosamine may be used to improve joint health. Environmental aids, including doggy "stairs" and ramps, remove some of the pressure on the affected joints and help pets to stay active.

Most cases of arthritis are natural consequences of aging that require management focusing on pain relief and facilitating ease of motion. Some dogs become so crippled their humans buy mobility carts for them. These devices, which attach to the hips, put your pooch on wheels.

So long as your pet is otherwise healthy, this is a reasonable approach to a debilitating, but not fatal ailment. Often called "dog wheelchairs," these units can be purchased at:

- www.handicappedpets.com
- www.k9carts.com
- eddieswheels.com.

The carts are adjustable, but when possible should be custom fit to ensure maximum mobility.

Luxating Patella

Dogs with a luxating patella experience repeated dislocations of the kneecap. The condition is most common in small and miniature breeds, but can happen with any dog, including the Shar-Pei.

Often owners don't realize there is an issue with their pet's knee joint until the dog jumps down, lands badly, and starts to limp or favor one leg. The condition may be genetic in origin or be the result of physical injury.

Any time you see your pet limping or seeming more fatigued than usual, have the dog checked out. Conditions like a luxating patella worsen over time.

Hypothyroidism

When a Shar-Pei suffers from hypothyroidism, the thyroid gland in the neck is not producing sufficient amounts of thyroxine, which controls the animal's metabolism.

Hair loss on the trunk, the back of the hind legs, and tail are the first signs of hypothyroidism. The skin may become flaky, and black patches of skin can appear. This may be followed by a loss of muscle mass, weight gain, and an overall sluggishness. The heart rate will be slow and the dog may be unusually sensitive to cold.

Blood tests are needed for a definitive diagnosis. The condition is not life-threatening, but the dog will need oral drugs for life. The preferred medication is a manmade version of the hormone called levothyroxine of L-thyroxine.

Canine Eye Care

Always check your Shar-Pei's eyes on a regular basis. As a part of good grooming, you want to keep the area in the corner of the eyes and along the muzzle free of discharge to prevent bacterial growth. Ask your vet for sterile eyewash or pre-moistened gauze pads to help with this chore. In cases of excessive discharge from the eyes, consider having the dog tested for environmental allergies.

Although dogs love to hang their heads out the window of the car on drives, this creates a ripe situation for an eye injury or even infection from blowing debris. If you don't want to deprive your dog of this simple pleasure, use a product called Doggles. These protective goggles for dogs are colorful and inexpensive at less than $20 / £12 per pair.

The most common eye infection in dogs, conjunctivitis, presents with redness around the eyes and a green or yellow discharge. Antibiotics are used to clear up the infection and the dog may have to wear the "cone of shame" collar to prevent injury from scratching during the healing process.

Entropion

Entropion is an abnormal condition of the eyelid, which turns inward, irritating the cornea. The condition becomes apparent in puppies within the first few weeks after birth. The little dogs squint to close their eyes and suffer excessive tearing.

This is a painful condition that must be treated immediately. A canine ophthalmologist or qualified veterinarian must intervene. The lids are tacked in place with stitches for a period of days or even weeks to correct the abnormality.

Sometimes the procedure must be performed a second time until the "fit" is correct. During healing, artificial tears must be put in the dog's eyes to prevent drying. Without this intervention, the puppy's eyesight can be compromised or lost.

Tacking is done in small puppies. If that doesn't resolve the problem, entropion surgery must be done. If tacks are needed in an older or adult dog, they will need entropion surgery, which must be done by an experienced and qualified veterinarian.

Retinal Dysplasia

Retinal dysplasia is a non-progressive eye disease caused by a genetic defect, a viral infection, or a deficiency of Vitamin A in the diet. There are three types:

- focal or multi-focal - Small folds develop in the retinal tissue. They may become less pronounced as the dog ages, but they may cause blind spots in the field of vision.

- geographic - Irregular or horseshoe-shaped lesions may be present instead of or alongside folded retinal tissue. This variation leads to visual impairment and possible blindness.

- complete - This form is accompanied by retinal detachment, causing blindness and secondary eye problems like cataracts or glaucoma.

The various forms of dysplasia cannot be detected with the naked eye. When the dog begins to exhibit clumsy behavior, owners realize something is wrong. The vet will use a retina scope to examine the eye, and you and your pet will be referred to a veterinary ophthalmologist.

There is no way to treat or reverse retinal dysplasia. Dogs with the condition should never be used for breeding. Most affected animals live full and healthy lives with necessary assistance and environmental aids as needed.

Glaucoma

With glaucoma, increased pressure in the eye prevents proper drainage of fluid. Glaucoma may develop spontaneously or as a complication of a shifted cataract. Dogs with glaucoma experience partial or total loss of vision within one year of diagnosis. Symptoms include swelling, excessive tearing, redness, and evident visual limitations. Suspected glaucoma requires immediate medical attention.

Allergies

Dogs can suffer from allergies just like humans. Anything that can touch the skin, be inhaled, or eaten has the potential to trigger an adverse reaction. Owners may first realize something is wrong if the dog begins to scratch or lick excessively, or in some cases to chew or bite the paws, tail, stomach, or hind legs.

In instances of airborne allergies, the dog may sneeze, cough, or experience watering eyes. Food allergies often trigger vomiting or diarrhea. Skin irritations may include rashes or hives. In short, your Shar-Pei can be absolutely miserable.

Negative reactions in the spring or fall can likely be traced to seasonal pollen. Fleas are often the culprits in warm weather. Food allergies can occur at any time, with the greatest offenders including beef, corn, wheat, soybeans and dairy products.

Allergy testing offers a definitive diagnosis and points toward environmental and dietary changes. The tests are expensive, costing $200+ / £120+. The dog may need medication or interventions like cool, soothing baths. In cases of food allergies, special diets are common.

Plastic food bowls can cause an acne-like inflammation on your dog's chin. Switch to stainless steel, glass, or ceramic dishes. Wash your pet's face with cool, clear water. If the rash doesn't begin to clear up, ask the vet for an antibiotic cream.

Skin Fold Infections

As we have discussed earlier, it is a myth that the Shar-Pei are prone to skin conditions (and must receive a great deal of preventive care) because of their wrinkles.

A great deal of preventive care is not necessary, just basic cleanliness, which is achieved by regular grooming and bathing when needed.

Remember that it is a fallacy about drying and powdering between wrinkles to prevent yeast infections. Adult dogs are not so wrinkly that this is necessary. They are more likely to get yeast skin infections in their ears and between toes.

Photo Credit: Georgette Schaefer of Yu Kou Shar-Pei

Shar-Pei Fever

This is a very complicated disorder which is not fully understood. Dogs with Shar-Pei Fever experience periodic fevers as high as 107° F / 416° C. (The normal range is 99.5° - 102.5° F / 37.5° – 39.1° C.) The hock joints swell and the dog exhibits lethargy, vomiting, diarrhea, and shallow breathing.

As a result of a study undertaken by Dr. Linda Tintle DVM about FSF, it is believed to be linked to the mutation that causes wrinkling and mucin production.

Cate Stewart of Nordic Star Shar-Pei has this advice: "Most people treat at home with a fever reducer. Vets unfamiliar with this disorder will treat for infection and that isn't the case. Unknowing owners can spend a lot of money trying to figure out what the problem is. Often their labs are normal during an episode of FSF. Their hock and/or the muzzle will swell and be very painful. Experienced owners give Benadryl and a quick-acting fever reducer. It is believed to be an immunity-based condition in which the body suddenly has a hyper immune (inflammatory) response.

"Please note that I have experience dealing with this disorder so I treat at home. Not everyone should. I recommend speaking to a veterinarian who is familiar with this disorder to discuss the best plan for treatment for your dog. Experienced owners can easily recognize this disorder but always consult a veterinarian if your dog is sick, as it could be something else! Never diagnose or treat a dog without veterinary approval."

Shar-Pei Auto-inflammatory Disease & Hyaluronan

Expert Linda J.M. Tintle, D.V.M. has kindly produced this more detailed explanation specifically for this book:

Familial Shar-Pei Fever (FSF) was introduced in the early 1990s as a term to identify a condition observed in some Shar-Pei that included renal amyloidosis and recurrent fever of unknown origin, similar to some humans affected with the inherited condition Familial Mediterranean Fever. Later research into the causes of FSF revealed that FSF was but one manifestation of a recently identified overarching inherited disease state in Shar-Pei called Shar-Pei Auto-inflammatory Disease (SPAID). FSF is only one of several possible phenotypic signs of SPAID, as is renal (or systemic) amyloidosis which can occur independently from FSF.

Shar-Pei produce excessive amounts of a substance called hyaluronan (HA). This causes their breed-specific wrinkled, thickened skin and has also been linked to SPAID. A mutation and copy number variation of a regulatory element upstream to the gene for hyaluronan synthase 2 leads to the overexpression of HA in Shar-Pei. Anytime there is a need for HA within the body, they may make as much as 10 times more than dogs of other breeds. This may lead to problems because HA is a dynamic molecule with important roles in the maintenance of health.

We all have HA but some Shar-Pei have too much of a good thing.

An intricate network of HA cables, along with other molecules, forms a mesh on the surfaces of cells and fills the spaces between cells, comprising the extracellular matrix (ECM). Networks of HA also cover the intestinal tract microvilli and line blood vessels (endothelial glycocalyx). HA can also be a viscous gel that is an important component of joint fluid and the vitreous that fills the eyeball. It also plays critical roles in the kidney and the control of hydration, taking advantage of the molecule's sponge-like ability to hold up to 1,000 times its molecular weight in water.

When it is first formed, HA is usually a very large molecule, one of the largest in the body. Frequently resynthesized, it is turned over rapidly and degraded into smaller fragments that are continuously recycled. The breakdown of a Shar-Pei's excessive HA into fragments for routine metabolism may also contribute to auto-inflammation and randomly triggered fever events.

The long molecule of HA functions as one of the most primitive sentinels of innate immunity. If it is damaged and broken into small fragments, the body senses these small pieces as "wrong" and sounds the alarm. It is a fundamental barrier molecule of the innate immune system. Small fragments of HA can trigger the release of powerful messengers of fever and inflammation. HA is necessary for and promotes wound healing. But in Shar-Pei, the screeching alarm signal may be out of proportion to the seriousness of the injury. They may then overreact to relatively minor insults. This can lead to episodic fever and chronic inflammation.

Familial Shar-Pei Fever is an episodic fever syndrome (39.4 - 41.7 degrees C) that may or may not be accompanied by joint (usually the tibiotarsal or hock joint/s) or muzzle swelling. Fevers typically last from just a few to 36 hours and if they last longer than 48 hours, a veterinarian should rule out underlying persistent triggers of fever, including infection. A veterinarian should be consulted at the time of the first episode, if the fever approaches or exceeds 41 degrees C, or if the episode is unusual for that individual. In very rare cases, the fever events can be life-threatening but most are self-limiting. Prompt treatment with aspirin or non-steroidal anti-inflammatory drugs will usually reduce fever and alleviate pain.

Some bacteria, yeast, insects and snakes secrete hyaluronidases. Hyaluronidases are enzymes that break down HA. These types of attacks can cause serious, dramatic and sometimes life-threatening problems for Shar-Pei.

Damage to HA that is lining blood vessels may contribute to the edema of chronic swollen hock syndrome as well as an acute necrotizing neutrophilic vasculitis syndrome (very similar to Streptococcal Toxic Shock Syndrome or STSS in humans) that may occur after an FSF event. The latter may cause extensive skin sloughing with high mortality in some dogs and requires prompt, aggressive veterinary treatment.

Hyaluronosis is the presence of excessive deposition of HA, often described by the more general term mucinosis in Shar-Pei. Shar-Pei have excessive production of HA from skin fibroblasts resulting in hereditary cutaneous hyaluronosis. This can result in lakes or vesicles of HA in the skin. Fragile bubbles of mucin may disrupt the normal skin architecture causing vesicular cutaneous hereditary hyaluronosis (vHCH) in some individuals.

Unfortunately, the selection for excess wrinkling and the heavy, padded muzzle (meatmouth) that persist into adulthood led to the selection of dogs for breeding that carried a high number of the mutations that cause excess production of HA. This inadvertently predisposed these dogs and their offspring to problems from auto-inflammatory disorders, some of which can cause death at relatively young ages from complications of high fever, kidney or liver failure, and infections. The vast majority of dogs have no ill effects but they remain at risk.

What can a Shar-Pei owner do with this knowledge? The answer lies in HA's ability to promote health and healing when it remains in its native, high-molecular weight state: Work to keep their HA healthy and undamaged and support their ability to respond appropriately to insults that may result in damage. Know what signs to look for that indicate serious problems and seek veterinary help swiftly when needed.

Feeding a high-quality diet rich in the building blocks of HA and supplying the necessary vitamins and minerals for building HA is important. N-acetyl-glucosamine is the backbone of the large HA molecule and if inadequately supplied, less healthful smaller molecules may form. Glucosamine is abundant in the connective and joint tissue found in cheaper cuts of meat and fish, as well as in homemade chicken soup stock. Magnesium is a requirement for HA synthesis and body stores may be depleted if it is inadequately supplied in the diet. HA is degraded by reactive oxidative species, so antioxidants may be helpful to prevent oxidative damage. HA is up-regulated by hyperglycemia (high blood sugar), so feeding a relatively low-carbohydrate diet with restricted snacking and avoiding over-feeding is suggested.

Keep their skin and ears clean and healthy. This is where regular, fanatical cleansing and grooming routines pay off handsomely. Very gently remove the opportunistic bacteria and yeast before they jump in and wreak havoc. Many Shar-Pei do not enjoy the bathtub and for these dogs, gently washing with a warm washcloth or microfiber cleaning cloth may be more successful.

Many Shar-Pei have very narrow (stenotic) ear canals. It is particularly important that these dogs receive preventive measures to keep the canals free of debris, infection and inflammation that may cause obstruction and pain.

Work closely with your veterinarian to manage the signs of auto-inflammation, including Shar-Pei Fever. It may be necessary to have aspirin or prescription non-steroidal anti-inflammatory medication available to you to administer for episodes of fever and inflammation like swollen hocks and/or muzzle. Prescription colchicine therapy may be needed to control the silent background inflammation that can lead to kidney or liver failure from reactive amyloidosis and to reduce the severity and frequency of fever events.

Some Shar-Pei develop gastrointestinal inflammation with chronic or intermittent diarrhea that requires veterinary assessment and treatment. Food intolerances in dogs that have intestinal inflammation are not uncommon, and dietary adjustments, medication and probiotics may help. Severe skin and ear infections may need microscopic examination, cytology, culture and sensitivity testing to identify appropriate therapy.

Abnormal lumps or thickening of the skin of Shar-Pei should be examined by fine needle aspirate and cytology and/or biopsy with histopathology. Mast cell cancer is unfortunately common in the breed, and is the great pretender and sometimes mistaken for chronic infection or less serious conditions. Mast cells are frequently found in areas of mucinosis and it can take expert opinion to differentiate this from mast cell cancer.

A strong partnership with your veterinarian will help identify problems early. At least annual first morning sample urinalysis, complete blood count (CBC), blood chemistry profile, and total T4 thyroid testing are recommended for most Shar-Pei and may be needed more frequently if there is evidence of chronic inflammation. Advanced testing may be needed to eliminate other causes of their symptoms.

A test quantifying the number of inherited genetic mutations in the regulation of HA production present in an individual Shar-Pei is under development. Increased number of mutated copies (higher copy number variation or CNV) has been shown to be associated with increased risk for SPAID (including FSF and amyloidosis). Because all Shar-Pei carry at least two mutations that can predispose to auto-inflammation, this test will be an additional aid in diagnosis that may shed light on their relative risk, and that will also help breeders avoid breeding high-risk carriers to one another.

Hemorrhagic Gastroenteritis

Any dog can develop hemorrhagic gastroenteritis (HGE), a frightening condition with a high mortality rate. If a dog does not receive immediate treatment, death can occur rapidly.

Symptoms of HGE include:

- profuse vomiting
- depression
- bloody diarrhea with a foul odor
- severe low blood volume resulting in fatal shock within 24 hours

The exact cause of HGE is unknown. The average age of onset is 2-4 years, and the condition often surfaces in otherwise healthy dogs. Approximately 15% of dogs that survive an attack will suffer a relapse. There is no definitive list of high-risk breeds. Those with a high incidence rate include:

- Miniature Poodles
- Miniature Schnauzers
- Yorkshire Terriers
- Dachshunds

The instant your dog vomits or passes blood, get the animal to the vet. Tests will rule out viral or bacterial infections, ulcers, parasites, cancer, and poisoning. An electrocardiogram and X-rays are also primary diagnostic tools for HGE.

The dog will need hospitalization and aggressive treatment with IV fluids and even a blood transfusion. Both steroids and antibiotics are used to prevent infection. If the dog survives, the animal should eat a bland diet for a week or more with only a gradual reintroduction of normal foods. In almost all cases the dog will eat a special diet for life with the use of a probiotic.

The acute phases of HGE last 2-3 days. With quick and aggressive treatment, many dogs recover well. Delayed intervention for any reason results in an extremely poor prognosis.

Breeding Shar-Pei

The decision to breed a dog like the Shar-Pei should only be undertaken for one reason — a desire to improve existing bloodlines and to help create the finest examples of the Shar-Pei currently extant. We are talking about animals that, when sold at pet quality, cost $500 to $2,000+ / £350 to £1,282+. A show-quality puppy starts at $1,000 / £650 and up. A breeding pair can easily be four times that amount.

Breeding pedigreed dogs is not a get-rich quick scheme, nor is it an inexpensive hobby. Before you even contemplate making such a commitment to living creatures, you must be an expert not only in living with and training a Shar-Pei, but in reliably pairing animals for the best genetic results.

The purpose of this book is not to educate potential breeders, but to introduce the Shar-Pei to potential owners. You have a great deal to learn before you can even consider becoming a breeder, but if that is your ultimate goal, start making friends in the Shar-Pei world now. Cultivating a mentor is an essential step toward owning and operating a successful, well-run kennel.

Chapter 8 - Interested in Showing Your Shar-Pei?

If you have purchased a show-quality Shar-Pei and are planning to enter the world of dog shows and the dog fancy, you have a whole education in front of you.

If you have not already done so, you will want to begin to attend dog shows and to make connections in the world of the dog fancy to acquire the training to participate with your dog, or to hire someone to show the animal for you.

Photo Credit: Bobbie Libman of Mikobi Shar-Pei

What Dogs are Qualified to Participate?

For a dog to participate in a dog show, it must be registered with the governing body for that exhibition. For instance, dogs registered with the American Kennel Club that are 6 months or older on the day of the show are eligible to enter AKC sponsored events. Spayed or neutered dogs are not eligible, nor are dogs with disqualifying faults according to the accepted standard for the breed.

Joining a Breed Club

When you attend a dog show, find out about joining a breed-specific club in your area. Such groups usually sponsor classes to teach the basics in handling and showing the breed or will have contacts to put you in touch with individual teachers.

Breed club membership is also important to learn the culture of the dog fancy and to meet people in the show world. You will begin by participating in smaller, local shows to learn the ropes before entering an event that will garner points toward sanctioned titles within a governing group's system.

There are also "fun matches" that a new dog owner can participate in open to dogs from 3-6 months of age. Here they can get an idea of how dog show judging takes place. It's also a great training ground for that future show prospect.

Hiring a Professional

It is not uncommon for people who own show-quality animals to hire professional handlers to work with the dogs, for a fee.

If you are interested in going this route, be sure to interview several handlers and to get a full schedule of their rates. Attend a show where they are working with a dog and watch them in action. Ask for references, and contact the people whose names you are given.

Entrusting a handler with the care of your dog is an enormous leap of faith. You want to be certain you have hired someone with whom you are completely comfortable and with whom your dog has an observable rapport.

Interview With An Expert - Bobbie Libman

In order to give you a glimpse into what is involved in showing your dog, we have interviewed Bobbie Libman, who has decades of experience she can share with us.

I wanted to interview you because it seems to me you have an interesting personal story to tell, given your success showing your Shar-Pei. Perhaps we could start by you telling us what achievements you have accomplished?

For the most part, I have bred, nurtured, evaluated and shown dogs from my own bloodlines. I have used stud dogs from other lines when I didn't have a male that wasn't too closely related to my bitch. I did purchase 2 dogs years ago who became champions as well. They were a very integral part of my current breeding program today.

In just about every litter I ever bred, I succeeded in championing at least one puppy from the litter. Breeding for a show dog for me is, and has always been, my main reason for breeding. I have had 3 dogs in the top 20 nationwide without ever leaving the state of California. I had a beautiful girl CH Mikobi's Millennium (Milli) who was invited to the inaugural Eukanuba Classic held in Florida. Unfortunately, I didn't attend.

I've also finished several champions from bred-by-exhibitor classes, for which I am the most proud. AKC awards the owners with a beautiful gold medallion.

I also was the proud breeder-owner of CH Mikobi's Hallelujah, who was the first horse coat bitch to finish her championship in the United States. She finished in less than 2 months, shortly after we achieved acceptance into the American Kennel Club in 1992.

I was also the proud owner of two Register of Merit dogs. To achieve a Register of Merit, a male has to have sired at least 10 champions, and a female has to have whelped at least 5 champions.

I'm sure a lot of readers think there's lots of mystery behind these dog shows, but how did it start for you and when?

I actually had my first show dog in 1970. It was a Great Dane. I only bred one litter. I hired a professional handler to show my boy CH Ranlyn's Representative. Because of other interests, I stopped showing and breeding a couple of years later.

It wasn't until 1987 that I got interested in showing the Chinese Shar-Pei. I purchased him from a reputable breeder, but didn't know anything about showing at the time. The breed wasn't AKC recognized until 1992, but in 1987 you could show at Chinese Shar-Pei Club of America shows. I saw an ad in the paper that there was a CSP dog show, so I decided to go. I was a total novice, but I tried to emulate what I saw other handlers do and worked with my puppy.

First, I checked the breed standard, and after much deliberation, I thought he had all the necessary qualities. When I got to the show, I was amazed at how many Shar-Pei there were. I entered him in the 4-6 month dog class. Much to my surprise, there were 10 other dogs in his class. Even more surprising, he won the class and then went on to win Best of Opposite Sex. Best of Breed went to a female. Needless to say, I was hooked.

When he turned 6 months old, I began entering him in classes where he was eligible to win championship points. He became a CSPCA champion at the age of 13 months. I'm attaching a photo of that very proud moment. I was very fortunate to have been successful with my very first owner-handled show dog.

I know a lot of readers of this book are just interested in owning a Shar-Pei and may not necessarily want to show their dogs, but to anybody who is interested, is it an impossible dream or can anybody start to show?

Anybody can show a dog. I highly recommend that, FIRST AND FOREMOST, you get an objective appraisal of your dog's qualities. To qualify as a show dog, it can't have any disqualifying faults. However, it's important you find a mentor who can honestly help you evaluate your dog.

I also advise to attend conformation classes in your area if possible, and be sure your dog is well socialized. Presentation and the dog's attitude are also very important factors. Shy and timid dogs usually don't do well at a dog show.

When you went to the shows did you have the hope or aim of winning?

Of course, you always hope your dog will win. If you have done all your homework and your dog is a good representative of the breed, you should walk in the ring with confidence and present your dog as best as possible. THERE IS NO PERFECT DOG, and a good handler will know how to hide the faults and show off the best traits.

What is it like to take part? Perhaps you could give us an insider's view behind the scenes?

I always found going to a dog show exciting. You should always think of it as fun. It will give you an opportunity to meet many people who are also fanciers of your particular breed, and try to learn as much as possible. Hopefully, you will find people who are willing to help. But it is still a competition, and whether you win or lose, you should always be a good sport. Remember, there is always another show and another judge and different competition. After a while, you will get to know which judges like a particular type or style of your breed.

How does an owner get to take part in the Westminster Dog Show – where do they start out?

The Westminster Dog Show used to require that in order to compete, your dog must already be a champion. The entry forms are sent out in October of the previous year, and the limit is usually reached that same day. Dogs that have been exhibited the previous year will automatically get their entries accepted. It's pretty difficult for a novice or amateur handler to get their entries in on time. Personally, I have always had a dog that qualified every year, but chose not to enter.

As an expert, what advice would you give to people who are looking to buy a Shar-Pei for show purposes?

Do your homework. Go to a REPUTABLE breeder. Talk to many breeders, and decide which one you have the most confidence in.

Most puppies are sold around 10-12 weeks old. They still have their baby teeth, so until their adult teeth come in, it's difficult to determine if their bite is going to be correct at 6 months old. Also, the testicles on males sometimes don't drop until after they are finished teething. Sometimes, males can be deemed monorchid (only one descended testicle). That would be a disqualification.

Some breeders guarantee a show dog and if the dog doesn't turn out (for whatever reason), they will replace it. Other breeders will sell the pup at a "pet" price, and if it is eligible to show at 6 months, they ask for the monetary difference between a companion puppy or a puppy with show potential.

There can be a huge difference between a 10- to 12-week-old pup and a 6-month-old pup. You would have to rely on the "educated guess" of your breeder to determine what will eventually grow into a "show dog" who can someday become a champion.

Bobbie Libman - HOUSE OF MIKOBI (AKC Breeder of Merit)
http://www.sharpeidogs.ca/mikobi

Chapter 9 – Shar-Pei and Older Age

It can be heartbreaking to watch your beloved pet grow older – he may develop health problems like arthritis, and he simply might not be as active as he once was.

Unfortunately, aging is a natural part of life that cannot be avoided. All you can do is learn how to provide for your Shar-Pei's needs as he ages so you can keep him with you for as long as possible.

What to Expect

Aging is a natural part of life for both humans and dogs. Sadly, dogs reach the end of their lives sooner than most humans do.

Once your Shar-Pei reaches the age of 8 years or so, he can be considered a "senior" dog.

At this point, you may need to start feeding him a dog food specially formulated for older dogs, and you may need to take some other precautions as well.

In order to properly care for your Shar-Pei as he ages, you might find it helpful to know what to expect. On this page, you will find a list of things to expect as your Shar-Pei dog starts to get older:

• Your dog may be less active than he was in his youth – he will likely still enjoy walks, but he may not last as long as he once did and he might take it at a slower pace.

• Your Shar-Pei's joints may start to give him trouble – check for signs of swelling and stiffness and consult your veterinarian with any problems.

• Your dog may sleep more than he once did – this is a natural sign of aging but it can also be a symptom of a health problem, so consult your vet if your dog's sleeping becomes excessive.

• Your dog may have a greater tendency to gain weight, so you will need to carefully monitor his diet to keep him from becoming obese in his old age.

• Your dog may have trouble walking or jumping, so keep an eye on your Shar-Pei if he has difficulty jumping, or if he starts dragging his back feet.

• Your dog's vision may no longer be as sharp as it once was, so your Shar-Pei may be predisposed to these problems.

• You may need to trim your Shar-Pei's nails more frequently if he doesn't spend as much time outside as he once did when he was younger.

•   Your dog may be more sensitive to extreme heat and cold, so make sure he has a comfortable place to lie down both inside and outside.

•   Your dog will develop gray hair around the face and muzzle – this may be less noticeable in Shar-Pei with a lighter coat.

While many of the signs mentioned above are natural side effects of aging, they can also be symptoms of serious health conditions.

If your dog develops any of these problems suddenly, consult your veterinarian immediately.

Caring for an Older Shar-Pei

When your Shar-Pei gets older, he may require different care than he did when he was younger.

The more you know about what to expect as your Shar-Pei ages, the better equipped you will be to provide him with the care he needs to remain healthy and mobile.

Here are some tips for caring for your Shar-Pei dog as he ages:

•   Schedule routine annual visits with your veterinarian to make sure your Shar-Pei is in good condition.

•   Consider switching to a dog food that is specially formulated for senior dogs – a food that is too high in calories may cause your dog to gain weight.

- Supplement your dog's diet with DHA and EPA fatty acids to help prevent joint stiffness and arthritis.

- Brush your Shar-Pei's teeth regularly to prevent periodontal diseases, which are fairly common in older dogs.

- Continue to exercise your dog on a regular basis – he may not be able to move as quickly, but you still need to keep him active to maintain joint and muscle health.

- Provide your Shar-Pei with soft bedding on which to sleep – the hard floor may aggravate his joints and worsen arthritis.

- Use ramps to get your dog into the car and onto the bed, if he is allowed, because he may no longer be able to jump.

- Consider putting down carpet or rugs on hard floors – slippery hardwood or tile flooring can be very problematic for arthritic dogs.

In addition to taking some of the precautions listed above in caring for your elderly Shar-Pei, you may want to familiarize yourself with some of the health conditions your dog is likely to develop in his old age.

Elderly dogs are also likely to exhibit certain changes in behavior, including:

- Confusion or disorientation
- Increased irritability
- Decreased responsiveness to commands
- Increase in vocalization (barking, whining, etc.)
- Heightened reaction to sound

- Increased aggression or protectiveness
- Changes in sleep habits
- Increase in house soiling accidents

As he ages, these tendencies may increase – he may also become more protective of you around strangers.

As your Shar-Pei gets older, you may find that he responds to your commands even less frequently than he used to.

The most important thing you can do for your senior dog is to schedule regular visits with your veterinarian. You should also, however, keep an eye out for signs of disease as your dog ages.

The following are common signs of disease in elderly dogs:

- Decreased appetite
- Increased thirst and urination
- Difficulty urinating/constipation
- Blood in the urine
- Difficulty breathing/coughing
- Vomiting or diarrhea
- Poor coat condition

If you notice your elderly Shar-Pei exhibiting any of these symptoms, you would be wise to seek veterinary care for your dog as soon as possible.

Euthanasia

The hardest decision any pet owner makes is helping a suffering animal to pass easily and humanely. I have been in this position, and even though I know my beloved companion died peacefully and with no pain, my own anguish was considerable. Thankfully, I was in the care of and accepting the advice and counsel of exceptional veterinary professionals.

This is the crucial component in the decision to euthanize an animal. For your own peace of mind, you must know that you have been given the best medical advice possible. My vet was not only knowledgeable and patient, but she was kind and forthright. I valued all of those qualities and hope you are as blessed as I was in the same situation.

But the bottom line is this. No one is in a position to judge you. No one. You must make the best decision that you can for your pet and for yourself. So long as you are acting from a position of love, respect and responsibility, whatever you do is "right."

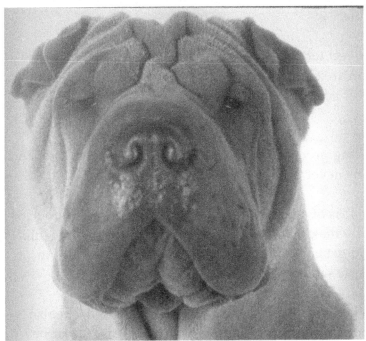

Photo Credit: Lynn and Michael Olds of Lava Kennels

Grieving a Lost Pet

Some humans have difficulty fully recognizing the terrible grief involved in losing a beloved canine friend.

There will be many who do not understand the close bond we humans can have with our dogs, which is often unlike any we have with our human counterparts.

Your friends may give you pitying looks and try to cheer you up, but if they have never experienced the loss of such a special connection themselves, they may also secretly think you are making too much fuss over "just a dog."

For some of us humans, the loss of a beloved dog is so painful that we decide never to share our lives with another, because the thought of going through the pain of such a loss is unbearable.

Expect to feel terribly sad, tearful and yes, depressed, because those who are close to their canine companions will feel their loss no less acutely than the loss of a human friend or life partner.

The grieving process can take some time to recover from, and some of us never totally recover.

After the loss of a family dog, first you need to take care of yourself by making certain that you remember to eat regular meals and get enough sleep, even though you will feel an almost eerie sense of loneliness.

Losing a beloved dog is a shock to the system that can also affect your concentration and your ability to find joy or be interested in participating in other activities that are a normal part of your daily life.

Other dogs, cats and pets in the home will also be grieving the loss of a companion and may display this by acting depressed, being off their food or showing little interest in play or games.

Therefore, you need to help guide your other pets through this grieving process by keeping them busy and interested, taking them for extra walks and finding ways to spend more time with them.

Wait Long Enough

Many people do not wait long enough before attempting to replace a lost pet and will immediately go to the local shelter and rescue a deserving dog. While this may help to distract you from your grieving process, this is not really fair to the new fur member of your family.

Bringing a new pet into a home that is depressed and grieving the loss of a long-time canine member may create behavioral problems for the new dog that will be faced with learning all about their new home, while also dealing with the unstable energy of the grieving family.

A better scenario would be to allow yourself the time to properly grieve by waiting a minimum of one month to allow yourself and your family to feel happier and more stable before deciding upon sharing your home with another dog.

Managing Health Care Costs

Thanks to advances in veterinary science, our pets now receive viable and effective treatments. The estimated annual cost for a medium-sized dog, including health care, is $650 / £387. (This does not include emergency care, advanced procedures, or consultations with specialists.)

The growing interest in pet insurance to help defray these costs is understandable. You can buy a policy covering accidents, illness, and hereditary and chronic conditions for $25 / £16.25 per month. Benefit caps and deductibles vary by company. To get rate quotes, investigate the following companies in the United States and the UK:

United States

http://www.24PetWatch.com
http://www.ASPCAPetInsurance.com
http://www.EmbracePetInsurance.com
http://www.PetsBest.com
http://www.PetInsurance.com

United Kingdom

http://www.Animalfriends.org.uk
http://www.Healthy-pets.co.uk
http://www.Petplan.co.uk

Afterword

Had it not been for the efforts of dedicated enthusiasts in the 1950s and 1960s, the Shar-Pei could have been an unexpected Cold War casualty. Seen as luxury items under the Communist regime in China, the dogs were killed in large numbers until a few were smuggled out to Hong Kong.

There, and as a result of importation to the United States and Great Britain, these unique animals survived to become one of the most popular dog breeds in the world today.

It would be wrong to characterize the Shar-Pei as an "easy" canine companion. They should never be someone's first dog. This breed requires understanding and insight from real dog lovers to get past their aloof and obstinate personality to the loyal and affectionate creature behind those passive and wise eyes.

Beyond the obvious appeal of the famous Shar-Pei wrinkles, there's something oddly distant and remote in this dog's expression, as if he knows deep secrets from ages past he has no intention of sharing with mere mortals. They are highly intelligent dogs, capable of doing almost anything, but only accepting of training on their own terms.

Quiet, clean, and on a whole undemanding, the Shar-Pei makes a surprisingly good apartment dog. Pairing him with other dogs, and with cats, is iffy given the breed's territorial instincts, and this is not a dog for a child. But as a companion to someone willing to understand his unique outlook, a Shar-Pei can be the dog of a lifetime.

Bonus Chapter 1 - Interview With Cate Stewart

Cate, thanks for doing this interview, can you tell us who you are and where you are based?

I live in Buffalo, Minnesota, USA, on a 40-acre hobby farm with my husband John.

I have been involved in this breed for 30 years. My involvement with this breed is widespread. My involvement includes being a member of the Chinese Shar-Pei Club of America (CSPCA), the Star of the North Shar-Pei club (SOTN) based in Minnesota. I am a licensed AKC judge of the Chinese Shar-Pei and an all-breed judge of Jr. Showmanship. I have taught both conformation classes and Jr. Handling classes. I am currently on the Board of Directors of the CSPCA and I have served on the Board of Directors for the SOTN. I am the Judges Education Chairman for the CSPCA, and I am also CHIC chairman for CSPCA. I am also involved in rescue. I currently show Shar-Pei and occasionally breed. I am an AKC Breeder of Merit.

What inspired you to become a breeder and did you start with the Shar-Pei?

My love of dogs was something I was born with. I became interested in showing and breeding as early as 5th grade. I read everything I could get my hands on about dogs, including showing and breeding dogs. As a child I would hold dog shows in my backyard for the neighbor dogs and I would act as the judge! This has been a lifelong affliction. I started in Jr. Showmanship at age 11. Shar-Pei was the first breed I bred. I bred my first litter in 1988. My "kennel name" is Nordic Star, which was established in 1986.

How did you progress to showing your Shar-Pei?

I bought my first Shar-Pei in 1985, a black short brush coat bitch. Her name was Ch, Coastal Bend's Hi-Hope Halley. I really didn't know much about the breed at the time. There wasn't much information out there. This was before email and the Internet. I thought she was beautiful and she conformed to the CSPCA breed standard so I started entering some rare breed shows. At this point they had not been accepted into AKC. She did well at the shows so I started entering her in the CSPCA shows. She did well in those as well and became a CSPCA champion. Halley was bred to Ch. Shir Du Bang in 1988, which produced my first litter. In 1988 I got a red brush coat bitch. Her name was Alpha Autumn Glo, Nordic Star call name "Autumn." She was a very special girl. She was an outstanding show dog, winning many very large specialty shows. She was a CSPCA champion and then when the Shar-Pei entered AKC in 1992 she earned an AKC championship. I showed her at Westminster the first year they were eligible and she received an award of merit. In those days the classes of Shar-Pei were quite large. If I remember correctly, around 40 were entered at Westminster that year.

I have bred, shown and owned many since then. I am currently showing GCH Nordic Star's In The Nick of Time, call name "Vita." She is a joy to show and is a lovely example of the breed. I plan to breed her soon in hopes of getting my next show dog.

My other very special "special" is GCH Destiny Texas Hold'm, Nordic Star call name "Deuce." Deuce was a top-ranked special for a few years running. Before retiring, his show career culminated by winning the CSPCA stop veteran of the year for 2012 and he also won Best Veteran at the 2012 CSPCA national specialty. Deuce, now 10, enjoys a life of leisure by watching his family and essentially doing whatever he wants.

What advice and tips could you offer to owners who might wish to follow your path?

Do your homework!! Find a knowledgeable breeder and mentor, learn as much as you can and never stop learning. If you plan to get a show dog, learn and understand the standard and start with a dog that most fits that standard. No matter if you show or are looking for a companion animal, find a dog who comes from a show breeder who does the proper health screenings.

I wish I would have had a mentor back when I started, seems I had to learn everything by experience and trial and error. I have met so many wonderful people in the breed, I have learned much through them as well. I have known many people since the early days and they remain my friends today. The knowledge and history held by the people who have been around since the early days of CSPCA and even AKC is so valuable. Talk to these people; no matter how long someone has been around, I know you will find what they have to say interesting. Never stop trying to learn and understand how we got to where we are today.

I know you are involved in the CSPCA, perhaps you could tell us a little more about the organization and its aims?

All parent breed clubs exist to encourage and promote the breeding and ownership of purebred dogs and to do everything possible to bring their natural qualities to perfection. The CSPCA is made up of people who love the breed, some show the dogs, some are involved in performance and some are pet owners. No matter a member's involvement, we all want what is in the best interest of this treasured breed. A breed club and its members are the steward of the breed and it is our responsibility to protect, maintain and improve the breeding and owning of Shar-Pei.

What types of people are buying a Shar-Pei?

All types of people have Shar-Pei. They are a breed that is very adaptable to whatever function you are interested in. They generally will be as active as you are. They do well next to you on the couch, in the show ring, or in a performance event their limits are endless. They are truly a versatile breed.

Are there some types of people that you suggest the Shar-Pei is not suitable for, perhaps families?

Yes. The Shar-Pei are intensely devoted to their owner(s). They were bred for eons to protect families and property. That instinct is very strong. They want to be with you, near you – that is when they are the happiest. If a family is looking for a dog to live outside in a kennel with minimal contact, this is not the breed for them. As with any breed of dog they depend on you for all of their needs. If one isn't able to consistently provide that, don't get a dog. I will qualify this by saying I know breeders who do maintain beautiful kennels which are climate controlled, clean and comfortable. These dogs also get daily exercise socialization and interaction; many also rotate through living in the home. When done in this manner a Shar-Pei can thrive in this environment as well. If the dog was given the choice, they just want to be with you.

Do they attract a lot of interest and curiosity from the public?

Yes, I think so; however, these days most people recognize the breed. When I first got the breed most had never seen one or heard of one. Their unique look is hard to resist.

What types of health issues can a Shar-Pei have and how do you deal with preventing these?

Unfortunately, as with any breed of dog, they can have health problems. Being knowledgeable of what they are and how to recognize and treat them is imperative. Know the pedigrees, including collateral dogs in that pedigree. Do what health screenings are available; I recommend doing the screenings set out by CHIC (canine health information center) for the Shar-Pei. Never buy from someone who cannot provide you with the parent's health screening documentation. At a minimum, they should have OFA or Penn hip evaluations, OFA elbow screenings and patellas certified free of luxation by a veterinarian.

Some of the common problems seen in the breed are entropion, chronic ear infections, hypothyroidism, and allergies, resulting in skin problems, higher incidence of certain cancers, familial Shar-Pei fever and renal amyloidosis. Doing the available health screenings, and careful and educated breeding, can help reduce these problems. However, despite the most careful breeding they can still happen, as they are inherent problems in the breed.

What is the typical temperament of a Shar-Pei so people know what to expect from their new pet?

Per the standard, "Regal, alert, intelligent, dignified, lordly, scowling, sober and snobbish essentially independent and somewhat standoffish with strangers, but extreme in his devotion to his family. The Shar-Pei stands firmly on the ground with a calm, confident stature."

This breed must be socialized from early puppyhood! Their nature is to be standoffish with strangers and even suspicious of them. Remembering they were bred to protect, so they aren't going to welcome a stranger into their circle at first – you have to earn it! Early and consistent socialization will help them be more accepting of strangers and new situations. I often tell people don't be offended if a Shar-Pei snubs you, they are just being a Shar-Pei. When touched by strangers they will usually shake themselves off as if to shake you off of them.

Do you have any special feeding routines or diet?

I feed my dogs twice a day. I feed a high-quality grain-free food. Just as people do, some dogs have special dietary needs or intolerances. You have to know what keeps your dog in the best condition and do that. It may take some trial and error. No one food fits all. If food or environmental allergies are a problem, I would recommend allergy testing and that you modify their diet accordingly. I am also not opposed to some table scraps with their regular diet as a treat. My dogs do well with some scraps as treats but not all dogs can tolerate that. If a dog is having frequent digestive problems consult with your veterinarian.

Can you offer advice to people looking to buy a Shar-Pei and how much should they be spending?

Again, do your homework. Get to know a breeder who can demonstrate to you the knowledge and commitment to health, temperament and the well-being of the dog for its life. The breeder of your dog should be available to answer your questions or help you learn about your dog for the entire life of your dog. Be cautious of people who breed only dogs to be sold as pets. These people, often known as backyard breeders, have one goal in mind: to sell you a puppy. Their goal is not to improve the breed. Often no health screenings have been done, they aren't knowledgeable about the breed and its potential problems, and they have little or no interest in the dog or the new owner once the puppy is purchased. Also be cautious of people claiming to have "rare colors" or claiming to have colors not listed on AKC registration choices. Anything that does not conform to the AKC written standard is a good guide of what to avoid. Prices can vary a lot. It isn't unusual to pay $1,000 to $1,500 for a "pet-quality" puppy or to pay $1,500–$3,000 for a show-potential puppy. Always get a written guarantee and contract from the breeder no matter the price. This goes for both pets and show prospects. A breeder with the best interest of the breed in mind will also require a spay or neuter contract on dogs/puppies sold as pets.

What colors and sizes are most popular?

There is only one AKC-recognized size of the Shar-Pei. "Miniature Shar-Pei" are not recognized by AKC or CSPCA. The Shar-Pei generally fall between 18-20 inches at the withers (top of shoulders) and weigh 45-60 pounds.

Both horse coat and brush coat are seen in this breed. They are equal in the show ring and one coat is not preferred over the other in the standard. Coat types and colors come down to personal preference.

Most common currently seen are brush coats, often fawn, red fawn or red. Despite that, both horse coat and brush coat come in a variety of colors both pigmented and dilute.

As a breed expert, are there any 'essential' tips you would like to share with new owners?

Over the years I have kept a running list of "tips for Shar-Pei owners" – it currently has 31 items on it. All of these are from my own experiences in 30 years with this breed. Too many to list here but as with any breed, know what you are getting into. Due to some of the health issues in the breed that can arise, if you live on a very tight budget I would not recommend this breed. Some of these issues can be very expensive to treat.

If you aren't looking for a dog who wants to be at your side at all times do not get a Shar-Pei. Have a lot of paper towels on hand and get used to having wet socks! They can be messy water drinkers.

Be prepared to have more than one Shar-Pei – no one can own only one. Once you have a Shar-Pei you will always have one. They have a magical thing about them only a Shar-Pei owner can understand.

Talk to breeders who have a proven track record of time and experience in this breed. Talk to people who have owned this breed. Don't rush into buying this or any breed. You are making a commitment to care for a living, social and at times demanding animal. If you can't devote yourself to that responsibility 100% don't get a dog until you can.

Cate Stewart of Nordic Star Shar-Pei
Email: nordicstarcsp@yahoo.com

Bonus Chapter 2 - Interview With Joy Bayliss

Joy, can you please introduce yourself by telling everyone who you are and where you live?

Joy Bayliss of the Tianshan Shar-Pei Kennel in the UK; I live in a small village near Louth in Lincolnshire.

You have had a lot of success at shows, including the highest possible achievement by winning at the world-famous Crufts dog show in the United Kingdom – what did you win there?

I bred & own The Crufts Best of Breed winner 2013 CH Tianshan Shine Rocco Baby, the only Horse Coat to win B.O.B at Crufts Since Challenge Certificate. I also bred his sire CH Tianshan Funky Red Rocco, & His Dam Tianshan Shining Dawn.

It must have been a long journey, how did it start for you with the Shar-Pei?

I started with a Black Horse Coat called Hector after seeing a photo in a book and I set about learning as much as I could about them; he was like no other dog I have ever met. He was so funny – I can remember walking him where some builders were working on an empty house, he ran in and came out with a carton of milk, he ran off in front of me, tipped it up, had a drink, then picked it back up and ran with it again. He did this for the entire walk; too smart for words – I was well and truly hooked.

At what point did you consider going to a show?

We then got our second Shar-Pei called Horace from a show kennel, the lady we had him from said I had a good eye for a dog and I should think about showing him. So I did lots of little fun shows and found I liked it so much.

I then got a little red horse coat called Mini. She was more of a show type, so I did bigger shows with her and we took her to Ireland where she won a Best of Breed, but it was quite a few years later before we had a big win like that one again.

Do you think most owners are intimidated by the thought they can't compete or that their dog will have no chance of winning?

Yes, I do think newcomers feel intimidated; there is so much to learn and many think it's a sprint, but in fact it's a marathon.

There is so much that goes into making a show dog – good socializing, ring training classes, then you have to stand in a ring where everyone else makes it look easy, and if you are not ready for all this it can put you off.

Where would someone reading this book begin?

The best thing you can do if you are planning to show your puppy is, once they have settled in their new home, work on socializing.

You can still safely socialize your puppy without walking the streets. This is how I do it – I take them in my car to the supermarket and sit outside with them on my lap so when people come out, they come over and fuss and chat to them. I get them to rub under the chin and then over their head and down their back, then give a little treat to the person to give to the puppy.

The work you put in at this stage of your puppy's life will shape them for life, so you need to get it right, take it slowly and build it up gently. Remember they are only babies and they need to know you are there for them and are in charge of every situation.

The Big One. Your puppy needs to be happy for a Judge to run their hands all over your puppy, so it is very important to get them used to this. So when your puppy is happy for you to be able to touch them all over, you can get your trusted friends to do the same. Start at the head, look in their ears and eyes, run your hands all down their back and down their legs.

It's a very good idea to show the judge your puppy's bite and pigment (see left), as some judges can be heavy handed, plus they can pass germs on, as they go in all the dog's mouths. Most judges are more than happy for you to show your own dog's bite, but do ask them if they have seen it all and don't rush it. You need to find a very good ring training class, and go a few times without the puppy to make sure it's a good class, plus it's good to have an idea on what to do before you take your puppy.

There are two ways to stand your dog for the judge: free standing and stacked; it's best to learn how to do both.

They should stand four square, as Annie is above. Place front legs first, then the back; do it in front of a mirror so you can see how they look.

Do it every day until they are very happy to do it, then you stand and stack your puppy and do the teeth and open (the bite) so you teach them separate, then put the two together. When stacking, it's best to slip four fingers under the collar so it does not look like they are being hung.

With free standing (see next page), you need to work at this with treats – a good ringcraft will show you how, and it can come later on in your show training but looks very nice when done well.

What tips and "secrets" can you give?

Be well organized, get to the show at least an hour before you are in the ring, this will give you and your dog time to settle down.

Make sure you have your ring number on; when you enter the ring, make an entrance, you only get one chance to make an impression. Remember the judge will look across the ring from time to time, so have your dog facing the judge even when you are relaxed. Better they see a nice head and not a bum, with you chatting to someone outside the ring. Keep an eye on the judge.

Before you set off, have your arm in an L shape (see below). It will help you keep in a straight line and have more control. Look at something in front of you, keep your eye on it and move towards it, say your dog's name then say move.

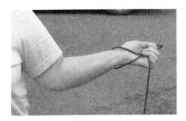

Never give your dog bate/treats when you are moving your dog, as your dog will look up at you and you need them to go in a straight line, or when the judge is going over your dog. Save the treat your dog loves the most for shows, not training, so you can get their attention even more so.

Don't get boxed in a corner, give yourself plenty of room by not standing too close to other exhibiters.

Always dress smart, wear good shoes you can run in, and ladies: a sports bra.

Hold your head up, try to look confident, look like a winner – you are a winner, the judge needs to know you can hold your own and show your dog off in the big ring. If you look too shy they may think you are not up to the job of representing your breed in the group ring.

Always have a cloth to wipe your dog's mouth dry; do this just before it's your turn to stand your dog for the judge, it makes showing the bite so much more easy, plus no judge wants to get a hand full of slobber.

Always warm your dog up before you go in the ring by having a little practice run.

Always take your dog to show in good clean condition.

Can you tell us how you get to even compete at Crufts and what is it like to take part?

To qualify for Crufts you need to win at least a 3rd in your class at a Championship show where Challenge certificates are on offer.

Just qualifying for Crufts and then taking part is just the best feeling, as there is such a buzz with a great atmosphere – it's what we all work for all year.

What types of owners are best suited to owning a Shar-Pei?

As a breeder, I feel the best type of owner would be someone who is kind and loving and will have time to give them all they need, as in mental stimulation, and will socialize them well, as they are so smart and need to have good interaction with their owners.

They are not a dog to be left all day when owners are at work, plus they are not a breed that can be put into boarding kennels, as they pine so much for the love of their lives, their owners.

The owner needs to be a strong leader, as they can be strong-willed, so not a good breed for the "Bunny hugger," as they soon learn how to rule the roost. They are very strong dogs and can pull their owners along if they are not trained and handled in the right way, so they may not be a good choice for first-time dog owners or people with very young children.

What can people expect when they become a new owner?

People who are new owners of this wonderful breed can expect unconditional love with a very strong bond. They are so loyal, they are a fun breed to live with and would put a smile on anyone's face. I could not live without mine, as they give so much in so many ways, truly the best breed in the world.

Joy & Richard Bayliss of Tianshan Shar Pei
http://www.tianshansharpei.co.uk/

Relevant Websites

Chinese Shar-Pei Club of America, Inc.
http://www.cspca.com

Chinese Shar-Pei Club of Canada
http://www.peiclub.com

The Shar-Pei Club of Great Britain
http://www.spcgb.org

Star of the North Chinese Shar-Pei Club
http://starofthenorthsharpeiclub.com/

Shar-Pei Club of Hong Kong
http://www.sharpeiclubhk.com

Shar-Pei Rescue of Great Britain
http://www.sharpeirescue.me.uk

Shar-Pei Rescue & Support Scotland
http://www.sharpeirescue-scotland.co.uk

Midland Shar-Pei Club
http://www.midlandsharpei.co.uk

The Berkshire Spur Chinese Shar-Pei Club
http://www.berkshirespurcspc.org

Centennial Shar-Pei Club
http://www.centennialsharpeiclub.org

Glossary

Abdomen – The surface area of a dog's body, lying between the chest and the hindquarters; also referred to as the belly.

Allergy – An abnormally sensitive reaction to substances including pollens, foods, or microorganisms. May be present in humans or animals with similar symptoms including, but not limited to, sneezing, itching, and skin rashes.

Anal glands – Glands located on either side of a dog's anus used to mark territory. May become blocked and require treatment by a veterinarian.

Arm – On a dog, the region between the shoulder and the elbow is referred to as the arm or the upper arm.

Artificial Insemination – The process by which semen is artificially introduced into the reproductive tract of a female dog for the purposes of a planned pregnancy.

Back – That portion of a dog's body that extends from the withers (or shoulder) to the croup (approximately the area where the back flows into the tail.)

Backyard breeder – Any person engaged in the casual breeding of purebred dogs with no regard to genetic quality or consideration of the breed standard is referred to as a backyard breeder.

Bitch – The appropriate term for a female dog.

Blooded – An accepted reference to a pedigreed dog.

Breed – A line or race of dogs selected and cultivated by man from a common gene pool to achieve and maintain a characteristic appearance and function.

Breed standard – A written "picture" of a perfect specimen of a given breed in terms of appearance, movement, and behavior as formulated by a parent organization, for example the American Kennel Club or in Great Britain, The Kennel Club.

Brows – The contours of the frontal bone that form ridges above a dog's eyes.

Buttocks – The hips or rump of a dog.

Castrate – The process of removing a male dog's testicles.

Chest – That portion of a dog's trunk or body encased by the ribs.

Coat – The hair covering a dog. Most breeds have both an outer coat and an undercoat.

Come into Season – The point at which a female dog becomes fertile for purposes of mating.

Congenital – Any quality, particularly an abnormality, present at birth.

Crate – Any portable container used to house a dog for transport or provided to a dog in the home as a "den."

Crossbred – Dogs are said to be crossbred when each of their parents is of a different breed.

Dam – A term for the female parent.

Dew Claw – The dew claw is an extra claw on the inside of the leg. It is a rudimentary fifth toe.

Euthanize – The act of relieving the suffering of a terminally ill animal by inducing a humane death, typically with an overdose of anesthesia.

Fancier – Any person with an exceptional interest in purebred dogs and the shows where they are exhibited.

Groom – To make a dog's coat neat by brushing, combing, or trimming.

Harness – A cloth or leather strap shaped to fit the shoulders and chest of a dog with a ring at the top for attaching a lead. An alternative to using a collar.

Haunch Bones – Terminology for the hip bones of a dog.

Haw – The membrane inside the corner of a dog's eye known as the third eyelid.

Head – The cranium and muzzle of a dog.

Hip Dysplasia – A condition in dogs due to a malformation of the hip resulting in painful and limited movement of varying degrees.

Hindquarters – The back portion of a dog's body including the pelvis, thighs, hocks, and paws.

Hock – Bones on the hind leg of a dog that form the joint between the second thigh and the metatarsus. Known as the dog's true heel.

Inbreeding – When two dogs of the same breed that are closely related mate.

Lead – Any strap, cord, or chain used to restrain or lead a dog. Typically attached to a collar or harness. Also called a leash.

Litter – The puppy or puppies from a single birth or "whelping."

Muzzle – That portion of a dog's head lying in front of the eyes and consisting of the nasal bone, nostrils, and jaws.

Neuter – To castrate or spay a dog, thus rendering them incapable of reproducing.

Pedigree – The written record of a pedigreed dog's genealogy. Should extend to three or more generations.

Puppy – Any dog of less than 12 months of age.

Separation Anxiety – The anxiety and stress suffered by a dog left alone for any period of time.

Sire – The accepted term for the male parent.

Spay – The surgery to remove a female dog's ovaries to prevent conception.

Whelping – Term for the act of giving birth puppies.

Withers – The highest point of a dog's shoulders.

Wrinkle – Any folding and loose skin on the forehead and foreface of a dog.

Index

garlic, 74

gastrointestinal upset, 58,
72, 121, 129

genitals, 38

gestational diabetes, 126

glaucoma, 132, 137

groomer, 89, 91, 92, 117

growths, 89, 126, 131

guard instincts, 22

guardian, 14

Han Dynasty, 13

harness, 94, 95, 186

hearing, 38, 113

heart, 51, 118, 125, 128, 134

heartworm, 124, 126

hemorrhagic
gastroenteritis (HGE),
146

hepatitis, 118

Hong Kong, 15, 16, 182

horse coat, 19, 33

housebroken, 1, 80

humidifer, 125

hunting, 14, 22, 26

hypothyroidism, 131, 134

identification, 49

insecticides, 57

intelligent, 13, 24, 33, 56, 67,
81, 95, 164

intestinal blockage, 95

irritability, 129

jaws, 14, 186

Kennel Club, 16, 50, 184

kennel cough, 124

kennels, 41, 44, 61

Lao Tzu, 29

learn, 24, 36, 41, 60, 67, 94,
128, 147

leash, 186

lethargy, 127, 139

lumps, 89, 126

lungs, 118, 125

luxating patella, 134

Macadamia nuts, 74

males, 26, 27, 87, 119

Mao Tse-tung, 15

mothballs, 57

mouth, 14, 17, 32, 89, 129,
131

Mushrooms, 74

neck, 30, 32, 93, 94, 134

neutered, 40, 45, 87, 119, 120

nostrils, 38, 186

Nylabones, 95, 114

obedience class, 24, 95

Onions, 74

parainfluenza, 118

parasites, 89, 119, 124, 125,
146

parvovirus, 24, 118

pets, 162

plants, 58

plaque, 128, 129

poisoning, 56, 146

praising, 62, 94

puppy, 186

puppy mill, 41

pyrethrum, 93

Raisins, 74

Raw chicken, 75